MW01504337

Praxis Special Education: Severe to Profound (5547) Study Guide

2024-2025

Pass the Praxis 5547 Exam with Detailed Content Review of Special Education Laws, IEP Implementation, Behavioral Management, Test-Taking Strategies, and Two Full-Length Practice Tests

Test Treasure Publication

Test Treasure
PUBLICATION

COPYRIGHT

All content, materials, and publications available on this website and through Test Treasure Publication's products, including but not limited to, study guides, flashcards, online materials, videos, graphics, logos, and text, are the property of Test Treasure Publication and are protected by United States and international copyright laws.

Copyright © 2024-2025 Test Treasure Publication. All rights reserved.

No part of these publications may be reproduced, distributed, or transmitted in any form or by any means, including photocopying, recording, or other electronic or mechanical methods, without the prior written permission of the publisher, except in the case of brief quotations embodied in critical reviews and certain other noncommercial uses permitted by copyright law.

Permissions

For permission requests, please write to the publisher, addressed "Attention: Permissions Coordinator," at the address below:

Test Treasure Publication

Email: support@testtreasure.com

Website: www.testtreasure.com

Unauthorized use or duplication of this material without express and written permission from this site's owner and/or author is strictly prohibited. Excerpts and links may be used, provided that full and clear credit is given to Test Treasure Publication with appropriate and specific direction to the original content.

Trademarks

All trademarks, service marks, and trade names used within this website and Test Treasure Publication's products are proprietary to Test Treasure Publication or other respective owners that have granted Test Treasure Publication the right and license to use such intellectual property.

Disclaimer

While every effort has been made to ensure the accuracy and completeness of the information contained in our products, Test Treasure Publication assumes no responsibility for errors, omissions, or contradictory interpretation of the subject matter herein. All information is provided "as is" without warranty of any kind.

Governing Law

This website is controlled by Test Treasure Publication from our offices located in the state of California, USA. It can be accessed by most countries around the world. As each country has laws that may differ from those of California, by accessing our website, you agree that the statutes and laws of California, without regard to the conflict of laws and the United Nations Convention on the International Sales of Goods, will apply to all matters relating to the use of this website and the purchase of any products or services through this site.

CONTENTS

INTRODUCTION

Education is a powerful tool, and for those working in **special education**, the ability to **support and uplift students with severe to profound disabilities** is both a privilege and a responsibility. The **Praxis Special Education: Severe to Profound (5547) Study Guide 2024-2025** has been carefully designed to help educators master the essential knowledge and skills needed to **excel on the Praxis 5547 exam** and, more importantly, in their teaching careers.

This guide serves as a **comprehensive resource**, offering in-depth coverage of key exam topics, **test-taking strategies**, and **practice questions** to ensure that educators are fully prepared. Whether you are a **prospective special education teacher**, a **current educator seeking certification**, or a **professional looking to deepen your expertise**, this study guide will equip you with the knowledge needed to **pass the Praxis 5547 exam with confidence**.

What This Guide Offers

Detailed Content Review – Covers all major areas tested in the exam, including **human development, instructional strategies, assessment, and legal considerations** in special education.

Study Schedules & Planning Advice – Provides **customizable study plans** to fit different learning styles and time constraints.

Test-Taking Strategies – Offers **practical tips and approaches** to handle different types of exam questions effectively.

Full-Length Practice Tests – Includes **two complete practice exams** with **100+ multiple-choice questions** and **detailed explanations** to enhance understanding.

Additional Resources – Recommends **online tools, professional organizations, and further reading materials** to supplement your preparation.

Who Should Use This Guide?

✔ **Aspiring Special Education Teachers** preparing for their Praxis certification.

✔ **Current Educators** looking to expand their expertise in severe and profound disabilities.

✔ **Education Students** who need a structured review of key special education concepts.

✔ **Professionals in Special Education Advocacy and Administration** seeking certification or enhanced knowledge.

How to Use This Guide Effectively

Start with the Exam Overview – Understand the **structure, format, and scoring** of the Praxis 5547 exam.

Follow a Study Plan – Choose from **short-term, mid-term, or long-term** study schedules based on your timeline.

Engage with the Content – Read through sections carefully, **take notes**, and

highlight key concepts for review.

 Practice with MCQs – Complete **200+ practice questions** to reinforce learning and assess readiness.

 Review Answer Explanations – Understanding why **each answer is correct or incorrect** is crucial for retention.

 Stay Consistent & Confident – Trust the process, **stay committed**, and build confidence as you progress.

Becoming a **special education professional** is more than just passing an exam—it is about **making a lasting impact** on students' lives. This guide not only prepares you for the Praxis 5547 exam but also **equips you with the essential knowledge and strategies** to provide **effective and compassionate instruction** to students with severe and profound disabilities.

Brief Overview of the Exam and Its Importance

What is the Praxis Special Education: Severe to Profound (5547) Exam?

The **Praxis Special Education: Severe to Profound (5547) Exam** is a standardized test designed to assess the knowledge and skills of **aspiring and current special education teachers** who work with students with **severe to profound disabilities**. This exam evaluates a candidate's ability to **develop instructional strategies, assess student needs, manage classroom behavior, and comply with special education laws and ethical practices**.

Passing the **Praxis 5547** is a crucial step for **educators seeking certification** in special education and demonstrates competency in **providing specialized support for students with severe disabilities**.

Exam Pattern and Key Details

Exam Component	Details
Test Name	Praxis Special Education: Severe to Profound (5547)
Administered By	Educational Testing Service (ETS)
Purpose	Certification for special education teachers focusing on students with severe/profound disabilities
Format	Multiple-Choice Questions (MCQs)
Total Number of Questions	Approximately 120
Time Duration	2 hours (120 minutes)
Scoring Scale	100 – 200
Passing Score	Varies by state (typically around 160-170)
Exam Mode	Computer-Based Test (CBT)
Availability	Offered at ETS-authorized testing centers and available for online proctoring in some locations
Test Fees	Varies based on location (typically between $130-$150)
Retake Policy	Candidates must wait **28 days** before retaking the exam

Exam Content Breakdown

The Praxis 5547 exam is structured around four key domains that **reflect essential competencies** for special education professionals:

Section	Topics Covered	Weightage
1. Human Development and Individualized Learning Differences	Theories of development, intellectual and developmental disabilities (IDD), impact on learning, individualized learning needs	25%
2. Planning and Instruction and the Learning Environment	IEP development, instructional strategies, classroom modifications, behavior management	30%
3. Assessment	Types of assessments, data collection, progress monitoring, legal considerations	20%
4. Ethical and Legal Practice, Professionalism, and Collaboration	Special education laws, ethics, collaboration with stakeholders, advocacy	25%

Importance of the Praxis Special Education: Severe to Profound (5547) Exam

State Certification Requirement: Many states require this exam for **special education teacher licensure**, ensuring educators are qualified to work with students with severe disabilities.

Demonstrates Professional Competence: Passing the Praxis 5547 demonstrates **proficiency in instructional methods, behavioral management, and legal compliance**, which are essential for **providing quality education to students with special needs**.

Enhances Career Opportunities: Many **school districts and special education programs** prefer or require candidates to have **Praxis certification** for employment and career advancement.

Ensures Quality Education for Students: Special education teachers play a **critical role** in **helping students with severe disabilities reach their potential**. This exam ensures educators are well-equipped to provide **tailored instruction and support**.

Prepares Educators for Real-World Scenarios: The exam covers **real-life classroom challenges, assessment strategies, and collaboration techniques**, helping educators **apply theoretical knowledge in practice**.

The **Praxis Special Education: Severe to Profound (5547) Exam** is a **gateway to a fulfilling career in special education**. It validates an educator's ability to **support students with significant disabilities, develop effective teaching plans**, and **advocate for student needs** within the legal framework of special education.

DETAILED CONTENT REVIEW

The **Praxis Special Education: Severe to Profound (5547) Exam** covers key concepts that educators must understand to provide effective instruction and support to students with severe to profound disabilities. This section provides a **comprehensive content review** of the **four major sections** tested on the exam, along with essential concepts, strategies, and best practices.

Section 1: Human Development and Individualized Learning Differences

Understanding how children develop and learn is crucial for educators working with students with severe and profound disabilities. This section covers **developmental theories, disabilities, and their impact on learning**.

1.1 Theories of Human Development

Several key developmental theories help explain how students learn and grow.

Theory	Key Concepts	Application in Special Education
Piaget's Cognitive Development Theory	Learning occurs in stages: Sensorimotor, Preoperational, Concrete Operational, and Formal Operational.	Adapt instruction based on cognitive abilities and modify abstract concepts for students with cognitive impairments.
Vygotsky's Sociocultural Theory	Learning occurs through social interaction and scaffolding.	Use **peer modeling, group activities, and visual aids** to enhance learning.
Erikson's Psychosocial Development	Individuals go through eight stages of social-emotional development.	Focus on building **trust, independence, and competence** in students through structured support.
Bronfenbrenner's Ecological Systems Theory	A child's development is influenced by multiple environments (family, school, community).	Promote collaboration between educators, families, and communities.

1.2 Understanding Intellectual and Developmental Disabilities (IDD)

Intellectual and developmental disabilities vary widely in severity and impact learning in different ways.

Disability	Key Characteristics	Educational Strategies
Autism Spectrum Disorder (ASD)	Difficulty with social interactions, communication, repetitive behaviors.	Use **visual schedules, structured routines, and social stories.**
Down Syndrome	Intellectual disability, speech delays, low muscle tone.	Implement **hands-on learning, repetition, and physical support tools.**
Cerebral Palsy	Impaired motor function, possible speech difficulties.	Provide **assistive devices, speech therapy, and flexible seating options.**
Fragile X Syndrome	Cognitive impairments, hyperactivity, anxiety.	Use **predictable routines, sensory-friendly environments, and calming techniques.**

1.3 Impact of Disabilities on Learning

- **Cognitive challenges** (e.g., processing delays, memory issues).

- **Motor difficulties** (e.g., challenges with writing, using learning tools).

- **Behavioral and social difficulties** (e.g., difficulties with peer interaction, emotional regulation).

- **Sensory processing issues** (e.g., hypersensitivity to noise, difficulty with textures).

Educational Adjustments:
✔ Use **visual schedules and structured routines**.
✔ Offer **alternative communication tools** for nonverbal students.
✔ Modify instruction based on the **individualized needs of students**.

1.4 Individualized Learning Needs

Every student has unique learning needs that require tailored instruction.

- **Differentiated Instruction:** Adjust lessons based on **cognitive levels and sensory needs**.

- **Use of Assistive Technology:** Tools like **AAC devices, screen readers, and adaptive keyboards** help students access learning.

- **Multi-Sensory Learning:** Engage **visual, auditory, kinesthetic, and tactile** learning modalities.

Section 2: Planning and Instruction and the Learning Environment

This section focuses on how to create an **effective learning environment**, develop **Individualized Education Programs (IEPs)**, and implement **instructional strategies**.

2.1 Developing Individualized Education Programs (IEPs)

The **IEP is a legally required document** that outlines a student's learning plan.

IEP Component	Purpose
Present Levels of Performance (PLAAFP)	Describes student's current skills and challenges.
Annual Goals	Defines specific, measurable goals for the student.
Accommodations & Modifications	Specifies changes in **instructional delivery and assessments**.
Related Services	Includes therapies such as **speech, occupational, and physical therapy**.
Transition Plan	Prepares older students for life after school (employment, independent living).

2.2 Instructional Strategies for Severe to Profound Disabilities

✔ **Task Analysis:** Breaking down skills into **small, manageable steps**.
✔ **Visual Supports:** Using **picture schedules, social stories, and graphic organizers**.
✔ **Repetition and Reinforcement:** Frequent **practice with rewards for progress**.
✔ **Sensory Integration:** Adapting instruction for **students with sensory processing challenges**.

2.3 Classroom and Environmental Modifications

- **Physical Layout:** Use **adaptive furniture, clear pathways for mobility devices.**

- **Quiet Zones:** Provide **low-stimulation areas for students with sensory sensitivities.**

- **Communication Supports:** Include **AAC devices, picture exchange systems.**

2.4 Behavioral Interventions and Classroom Management

✔ Implement **Functional Behavior Assessments (FBA)** to identify causes of challenging behaviors.
✔ Develop **Behavior Intervention Plans (BIP)** with **positive reinforcement strategies.**
✔ Use **Applied Behavior Analysis (ABA)** techniques for reinforcement.

Section 3: Assessment

Assessment helps track **student progress and guide instruction.**

3.1 Types of Assessments in Special Education

Assessment Type	Purpose
Diagnostic Assessments	Identify student's strengths and weaknesses before instruction.
Formative Assessments	Ongoing checks during learning (e.g., teacher observations, quizzes).
Summative Assessments	End-of-unit or year evaluations (e.g., performance-based assessments).
Functional Assessments	Measure life skills and independence.

3.2 Assessing Students with Severe to Profound Disabilities

✔ **Portfolios** – Collect work samples over time.

✔ **Observation-Based Assessments** – Record real-time performance.

✔ **Performance-Based Tasks** – Assess **life skills and communication abilities**.

3.3 Data Collection and Progress Monitoring

✔ **ABC (Antecedent-Behavior-Consequence) Charts** to analyze behaviors.

✔ **Frequency and Duration Recording** for tracking progress on IEP goals.

✔ **Technology-Based Data Collection** tools like **apps for real-time tracking**.

Section 4: Ethical and Legal Practice, Professionalism, and Collaboration

Understanding **legal requirements and ethical considerations** is crucial in special education.

4.1 Special Education Laws and Regulations

Law	Key Provisions
Individuals with Disabilities Education Act (IDEA)	Guarantees FAPE, LRE, and IEPs for students with disabilities.
Americans with Disabilities Act (ADA)	Ensures accessibility and accommodations in public spaces.
Section 504 of the Rehabilitation Act	Provides accommodations for students with disabilities in schools.

4.2 Ethical Responsibilities in Special Education

✔ **Confidentiality:** Protecting **student records** and privacy.

✔ **Advocacy:** Ensuring **students receive appropriate supports**.

✔ **Equity:** Providing **fair access to education for all students**.

4.3 Collaboration with Stakeholders

✔ **Family Involvement:** Engaging parents in the IEP process.

✔ **Interdisciplinary Teams:** Working with **therapists, specialists, and general educators**.

✔ **Community Resources:** Connecting families with **external support programs**.

4.4 Advocacy and Professional Development

✔ Attend **conferences, workshops, and training** to stay updated.

✔ Join **special education associations** for networking and resources.

✔ Engage in **continuous learning** to improve teaching strategies.

This **detailed content review** provides **theoretical knowledge and practical applications** to help educators **succeed in the Praxis Special Education: Severe to Profound (5547) exam** and **enhance their teaching effectiveness**.

STUDY SCHEDULES AND PLANNING ADVICE

Preparing for the **Praxis Special Education: Severe to Profound (5547) Exam** requires a **structured study plan** to ensure success. Every candidate has a different timeline based on their availability, prior knowledge, and study habits. This section provides **customizable study schedules** and **effective planning strategies** to help candidates make the most of their preparation time.

Choosing the Right Study Plan

Before creating a study schedule, ask yourself the following questions:

How much time do I have before the exam?

How familiar am I with the exam topics?

How many hours can I realistically dedicate per week?

Do I need more time for **practice tests** and **reviewing weak areas**?

Based on your answers, choose from one of the following study plans:

4-Week Intensive Study Plan (Best for Last-Minute Test-Takers)

This plan is ideal for **candidates with limited time** who need a **focused and efficient** study approach.

Week	Study Goals
Week 1	Read the **Exam Overview** and take a **diagnostic test** to identify strengths and weaknesses. Start **Section 1: Human Development and Individualized Learning Differences** and take notes on key concepts.
Week 2	Study **Section 2: Planning and Instruction and the Learning Environment** and focus on IEPs, **instructional strategies, and behavior management**. Complete practice questions for both Sections 1 and 2.
Week 3	Study **Section 3: Assessment** and **Section 4: Ethical and Legal Practices**. Take **timed quizzes** to improve speed and accuracy.
Week 4	Take a **full-length practice test**, review mistakes, and **focus on weak areas**. Revisit key concepts and reinforce learning with **flashcards and summary notes**.

✔ **Tip:** Since this schedule is fast-paced, focus on **high-yield topics** and practice **active recall** to retain information effectively.

8-Week Balanced Study Plan (Recommended for Most Candidates)

This plan provides **a structured yet flexible approach**, allowing candidates to study at a **steady pace**.

Week	Study Goals
Weeks 1-2	Read the **Exam Overview** and take a **diagnostic test**. Study **Section 1: Human Development and Individualized Learning Differences**. Take notes, highlight key theories, and complete practice questions.
Weeks 3-4	Study **Section 2: Planning and Instruction and the Learning Environment**. Focus on IEPs, **instructional techniques, and classroom management strategies**. Complete **weekly quizzes** to reinforce learning.
Weeks 5-6	Study **Section 3: Assessment** and **Section 4: Ethical and Legal Practices**. Learn about **special education laws, compliance, and collaboration**. Review past quiz results and track progress.
Weeks 7-8	Take **two full-length practice tests** under timed conditions. Review incorrect answers, refine **test-taking strategies**, and reinforce **difficult concepts**.

✔ **Tip:** Use a **mix of study methods** like flashcards, quizzes, group discussions, and real-world applications to deepen understanding.

12-Week Extended Study Plan (Best for In-Depth Preparation)

This plan is suitable for **candidates who prefer a slower, more comprehensive study approach**.

Week Range	Study Goals
Weeks 1-4	Study **Section 1: Human Development and Individualized Learning Differences** in detail. Focus on theories of development, intellectual disabilities, and individualized learning strategies. Complete weekly practice questions.
Weeks 5-8	Study **Section 2: Planning and Instruction and the Learning Environment**. Take **detailed notes on** IEPs, instructional techniques, and classroom modifications. Complete **weekly quizzes** and review progress.
Weeks 9-10	Study **Section 3: Assessment** and **Section 4: Ethical and Legal Practices**. Deep dive into **assessment tools, data collection methods, and special education laws**.
Weeks 11-12	Take **multiple full-length practice tests**, analyze mistakes, and revisit **trouble areas**. Review key concepts, focus on weak points, and build confidence.

✔ **Tip:** For long-term studying, use **spaced repetition** to reinforce concepts over time rather than cramming information at the last minute.

General Study Tips for Success

1. Create a Study Routine

* Set **specific study hours** each day to build consistency.

* Use a **planner or digital calendar** to keep track of study goals.

* Find a **quiet, distraction-free environment** for studying.

2. Use Active Learning Strategies

* **Summarize concepts in your own words** rather than just reading.

* Teach concepts to someone else to **reinforce learning**.

* Create **flashcards** for key terms, special education laws, and teaching strategies.

3. Track Progress and Adjust Accordingly

* Take **practice quizzes** regularly to measure progress.

* Identify weak areas and **spend more time reviewing them**.

* Use **study logs or reflection journals** to document learning.

4. Develop Effective Test-Taking Strategies

- **Read all answer choices carefully** before selecting the best response.

- **Eliminate incorrect options** to improve accuracy.

- Manage time wisely—don't spend too much time on one question.

- Answer **easier questions first** and return to harder ones later.

5. Utilize Additional Resources

- Explore **ETS Praxis study materials** and official practice tests.

- Join **special education forums and online communities** for support.

- Watch **educational videos** on key topics for visual reinforcement.

Final Week Before the Exam: Last-Minute Checklist

✔ Review summary notes and key concepts.
✔ Take at least one full-length practice test under timed conditions.
✔ Focus on test-taking strategies and time management.
✔ Get plenty of rest and stay confident!

A well-planned study schedule can make the difference between **stressful last-minute cramming** and **confident test performance**. By following the **structured study plans and strategies** provided in this guide, you will be well-prepared to **pass the Praxis Special Education: Severe to Profound (5547) Exam and advance your career in special education**.

FREQUENTLY ASKED QUESTIONS

To help candidates feel **fully prepared** for the **Praxis Special Education: Severe to Profound (5547) Exam**, we've compiled a list of **frequently asked questions** that cover key concerns about the exam format, preparation strategies, study resources, and test-day tips.

1. About the Exam

Q1: What is the Praxis Special Education: Severe to Profound (5547) Exam?

The **Praxis Special Education: Severe to Profound (5547) Exam** is a standardized test designed to assess an educator's knowledge and skills in **working with students who have severe to profound disabilities**. It is used by many states as part of the certification requirements for **special education teachers**.

Q2: Who administers the Praxis 5547 exam?

The **Educational Testing Service (ETS)** administers the Praxis exams. It is responsible for developing the test, scoring, and reporting results to candidates and their respective state licensing boards.

Q3: How many questions are on the exam?

The Praxis 5547 exam consists of **approximately 120 multiple-choice questions**. These questions cover a variety of topics related to **special education strategies, assessment, instructional planning, legal compliance, and student development**.

Q4: How much time do I have to complete the test?

The total time allotted for the exam is **2 hours (120 minutes)**. Candidates must manage their time effectively to complete all questions within this period.

Q5: What topics are covered in the exam?

The exam is divided into **four key sections**:

Human Development and Individualized Learning Differences – Covers theories of development, disabilities, and individualized learning strategies.
Planning and Instruction and the Learning Environment – Focuses on **IEPs, instructional strategies, classroom modifications, and behavior management**.
Assessment – Covers **different types of assessments, progress monitoring, and legal requirements**.
Ethical and Legal Practice, Professionalism, and Collaboration – Covers **special education laws, professional responsibilities, and stakeholder collaboration**.

2. Exam Preparation

Q6: How should I start preparing for the Praxis 5547 exam?

Start by:
- ✔ Reviewing the **exam structure and content outline**.
- ✔ Taking a **diagnostic test** to identify strengths and weaknesses.
- ✔ Following a **structured study plan** (4-week, 8-week, or 12-week).
- ✔ Practicing with **full-length practice tests and quizzes**.

Q7: What are the best study resources for this exam?

Some of the best study resources include:

This **study guide**, which includes **detailed content review, practice questions, and test-taking strategies**.

The **ETS Praxis website**, which offers official study materials and sample questions.

Online courses and video tutorials on **special education teaching strategies**.

Flashcards and quiz apps to **reinforce key concepts**.

Q8: How many hours should I study for the exam?

The amount of study time depends on your familiarity with the content:

- **4-Week Plan** (for last-minute preparation): 10-12 hours per week.

- **8-Week Plan** (recommended for most candidates): 6-8 hours per week.

- **12-Week Plan** (for in-depth preparation): 4-6 hours per week.

Q9: How many practice tests should I take?

Taking at least **two full-length practice tests** is recommended. These tests help improve **time management, question analysis, and confidence** before the actual exam.

3. Test-Day Essentials

Q10: What should I bring to the testing center?

On test day, you should bring:
✔ **Valid identification** (government-issued ID with your name matching your Praxis registration).
✔ **ETS Admission Ticket** (if required by the test center).
✔ **Acceptable writing tools** (if a paper-based test is being administered).
 DO NOT bring study materials, electronics, or personal items inside the testing room.

Q11: Can I take breaks during the exam?

There are **no scheduled breaks** during the 2-hour exam. If you take an unscheduled break, the exam timer will continue running.

Q12: How is the Praxis 5547 exam scored?

The exam is scored on a scale of **100–200 points**. The **passing score varies by state** but typically falls between **160-170**. Your raw score (number of correct answers) is converted into a scaled score.

Q13: When will I receive my test results?

Unofficial scores may be available **immediately** after the exam for multiple-choice sections. Official scores are usually **released within 10-16 days** via the **ETS Praxis account**.

4. Retaking the Exam

Q14: What happens if I don't pass the exam?

If you don't pass, you can **retake the exam after a 28-day waiting period**. Use this time to:
✔ Review your **score report** to identify weak areas.
✔ Adjust your **study strategy** to focus on lower-scoring topics.
✔ Take additional **practice tests and quizzes** to build confidence.

Q15: How many times can I take the Praxis 5547 exam?

There is no limit to the number of times you can take the exam, but you must wait **28 days between attempts**.

5. Career and Certification Questions

Q16: Do all states require the Praxis 5547 exam for special education certification?

Not all states require the **Praxis 5547** specifically. Some states use alternative exams or require multiple Praxis exams. **Check with your state's Department of Education** for specific requirements.

Q17: Will passing the Praxis 5547 guarantee me a teaching job?

Passing the Praxis 5547 exam is an important **step toward licensure**, but employment also depends on:

✔ **State certification requirements.**

✔ **Job availability in special education programs.**

✔ **Your teaching experience and qualifications.**

Q18: What are the career opportunities after passing the Praxis 5547?

Passing the exam qualifies you for roles such as:

Special Education Teacher (Severe Disabilities).

IEP Coordinator or Special Education Case Manager.

Behavior Intervention Specialist.

Assistive Technology Specialist.

School Administrator or Special Education Consultant (with additional experience).

Final Exam-Day Tips

Arrive early at the testing center to avoid last-minute stress.

Read all questions carefully and eliminate incorrect answer choices.

Manage your time wisely—don't spend too much time on one question.
Stay calm and confident—trust your preparation!

The **Praxis Special Education: Severe to Profound (5547) Exam** is a key milestone for **educators specializing in severe disabilities**. With **effective preparation, the right resources, and a strategic study plan**, passing the exam is **completely achievable**.

1

HUMAN DEVELOPMENT AND LEARNING DIFFERENCES

Developmental Theory Foundations

Human development serves as the bedrock for understanding how individuals learn and grow, and it is especially important when working with students who have severe to profound disabilities. This chapter explores some of the major developmental theories and their specific relevance to special education, focusing on the frameworks provided by Jean Piaget, Lev Vygotsky, and Erik Erikson. These theories offer valuable insights into cognitive, social, and emotional development, which can directly inform instructional strategies and interventions.

Piaget's theory of cognitive development suggests that children progress through distinct stages of intellectual growth, each characterized by unique ways of thinking and understanding the world. These stages are: sensorimotor (birth to 2 years), preoperational (2 to 7 years), concrete operational (7 to 11 years), and formal operational (12 years and beyond). While Piaget's original model was designed for typically developing children, certain elements can be adapted and applied to students with significant cognitive impairments.

For example, students with severe to profound disabilities may remain in the sensorimotor stage for an extended period, learning primarily through sensory experiences and motor actions. Educators working with these students can create learning environments rich in sensory stimulation, such as tactile objects, visual aids, and auditory cues. Activities might involve exploring different textures, manipulating simple toys, or responding to music and movement. The focus is on building basic sensorimotor skills, like reaching, grasping, and tracking objects, which form the foundation for later cognitive development.

Furthermore, Piaget's concept of object permanence – the understanding that objects continue to exist even when they are out of sight – is crucial for students with disabilities. Activities designed to promote object permanence, such as hiding a favorite toy under a blanket and encouraging the student to find it, can help develop cognitive awareness and understanding. It is essential to adapt these activities to meet the individual needs and abilities of each student, providing appropriate levels of support and challenge.

Vygotsky's sociocultural theory highlights the role of social interaction and cultural context in shaping cognitive development. Unlike Piaget, who emphasized individual exploration, Vygotsky believed that learning occurs primarily through social interactions with more knowledgeable others. Key concepts in Vygotsky's theory include the Zone of Proximal Development (ZPD) and scaffolding. The ZPD refers to the gap between what a learner can do independently and what they can achieve with guidance and support. Scaffolding involves providing temporary assistance to help learners bridge this gap and master new skills.

In special education, Vygotsky's theory suggests that educators should act as facilitators, guiding students through their ZPD by providing appropriate support and challenges. For students with severe to profound disabilities, this might involve breaking down complex tasks into smaller, more manageable steps, providing clear and concise instructions, and offering ongoing feedback and encouragement. Peer tutoring and cooperative learning activities can also be valuable, allowing students to learn from and support one another.

For example, consider a student learning to use an augmentative and alternative communication (AAC) device. The educator might begin by modeling how to select and activate different symbols on the device, gradually fading their support as the student becomes more proficient. Peer interactions can also be incorporated, with classmates helping the student to practice using the AAC device in social situations. The teacher can also design activities in which students can work together to achieve a common learning goal. In this case, the student with the AAC device can actively participate and contribute to the group.

Another crucial aspect of Vygotsky's theory is the importance of language in cognitive development. Language serves as a tool for thought, allowing individuals to internalize and organize their experiences. For students with limited verbal communication skills, alternative forms of communication, such as sign language, visual aids, or AAC devices, can play a vital role in supporting cognitive development and social interaction. Educators should create communication-rich environments that encourage students to express themselves and interact with others.

Erikson's theory of psychosocial development focuses on the social and emotional challenges individuals face at different stages of life. Erikson proposed eight stages, each characterized by a specific conflict or crisis that must be resolved for healthy development to occur. These stages are: trust vs. mistrust (birth to 1 year), autonomy vs. shame and doubt (2 to 3 years), initiative vs. guilt (3 to 5 years), industry vs. inferiority (6 to 12 years), identity vs. role confusion (12 to 18 years), intimacy vs. isolation (young adulthood), generativity vs. stagnation (middle adulthood), and integrity vs. despair (late adulthood).

While Erikson's stages are typically associated with specific age ranges, students with severe to profound disabilities may experience these stages differently and may require ongoing support to navigate the associated challenges. For instance, establishing trust is especially critical for students with disabilities, who may rely heavily on caregivers and educators for their physical and emotional needs. Creating a safe, predictable, and nurturing environment can help these students develop a sense of trust and security.

Similarly, promoting autonomy and independence is essential for students with disabilities, even if their abilities are limited. Educators can provide opportunities for students to make choices, express preferences, and participate in daily routines to the best of their abilities. Adaptive equipment, assistive technology, and individualized support can help students overcome physical and cognitive barriers and develop a sense of self-efficacy.

Furthermore, addressing issues of identity and self-esteem is crucial for students with disabilities, who may face societal stigma and discrimination. Educators can foster a positive self-image by focusing on students' strengths and abilities, providing opportunities for success, and promoting social inclusion. Encouraging students to participate in extracurricular activities, develop hobbies, and build friendships can also contribute to their overall well-being and sense of belonging.

Comparing these theoretical approaches, we see both commonalities and differences. Piaget emphasizes individual cognitive construction, while Vygotsky highlights the role of social interaction. Erikson focuses on social-emotional development across the lifespan. However, all three theories underscore the importance of understanding the developmental needs of each student and providing appropriate support and challenges.

Applying these theories in the classroom requires a flexible and individualized approach. Educators must assess students' current developmental levels, identify their strengths and weaknesses, and create learning experiences that are tailored to their specific needs. This might involve adapting instructional materials, modifying classroom routines, providing assistive technology, or collaborating with other professionals, such as therapists and counselors.

Consider a student with significant physical and cognitive disabilities who is working on developing basic communication skills. Drawing on Piaget's theory, the educator might provide sensory-rich experiences to stimulate the student's cognitive development. Using Vygotsky's framework, the educator might work closely with the student, providing scaffolding and support to help them learn to use an AAC device. Incorporating Erikson's principles, the educator would focus on building trust and promoting autonomy, allowing the student to make choices and express preferences whenever possible.

In another scenario, a student with autism spectrum disorder (ASD) and intellectual disability may struggle with social interaction and communication. Applying Vygotsky's theory, the educator might facilitate peer interactions and social skills training, providing opportunities for the student to practice social skills in a supportive environment. Using Erikson's framework, the educator would focus on building the student's self-esteem and promoting social inclusion, helping them to develop a sense of belonging and acceptance.

Understanding developmental trajectories is essential for designing effective interventions and promoting positive outcomes for students with severe to profound disabilities. By grounding their practice in established developmental theories, educators can create learning environments that are responsive to the unique needs of each student, fostering their cognitive, social, and emotional growth. This includes ongoing assessment, individualized instruction, and collaboration with families and other professionals. The goal is to empower students to reach their fullest potential and lead meaningful, fulfilling lives.

Intellectual and Developmental Disability Landscape

The landscape of Intellectual and Developmental Disabilities (IDD) is varied, requiring an understanding of clinical definitions, classification systems, and the underlying biological factors that contribute to these conditions. IDD represents a group of conditions that start during development, may impact intellectual, social, and adaptive functioning and include deficits in conceptual, social, and practical skills. It is essential to approach the study of IDD with both scientific rigor and a deep sense of empathy, appreciating the unique strengths and possibilities within each person.

To begin, it is vital to establish clear definitions and diagnostic criteria for IDD. Intellectual disability is characterized by substantial limitations in both intellectual functioning and adaptive behavior, which covers many everyday social and practical skills. These limitations must begin before the age of 18. Diagnostic criteria, as outlined in the Diagnostic and Statistical Manual of Mental Disorders, 5th Edition (DSM-5), involve standardized intelligence testing that yields an IQ score significantly below average (typically two standard deviations below the mean, or approximately 70 or below), alongside significant deficits or limitations in adaptive functioning. Adaptive behavior is assessed across three domains: conceptual (e.g., memory, language, reading, writing, math, reasoning, knowledge), social (e.g., empathy, interpersonal communication skills, friendship abilities, social judgment), and practical (e.g., personal care, job responsibilities, money management, recreation, organizing school and work tasks) skills. Deficits in adaptive functioning must be present in all three domains for a diagnosis of intellectual disability to be made.

Developmental disabilities encompass a broader array of conditions that arise during the developmental period, which extends from birth to age 22. These disabilities can be intellectual, physical, or both, and they may affect language, learning, mobility, self-care, and independent living. Examples of developmental disabilities other than intellectual disability include autism spectrum disorder (ASD), cerebral palsy, Down syndrome, and sensory impairments. It is crucial to recognize that some individuals may have co-occurring intellectual and developmental disabilities, adding complexity to their needs and support requirements.

Classification systems further refine our understanding of IDD by categorizing individuals based on the severity of their impairments. Intellectual disability, for instance, is classified into varying degrees of severity: mild, moderate, severe, and profound. These classifications are based on adaptive functioning, rather than IQ scores alone, reflecting the understanding that adaptive behavior is a more direct indicator of an individual's ability to function in daily life.

- **Mild IDD:** Individuals with mild IDD may have some difficulties in learning and academic skills. As adults, those with mild IDD can often live independently with some support, such as help with budgeting or job coaching.

- **Moderate IDD:** Those with moderate IDD demonstrate more pronounced delays in cognitive and adaptive skills. They need more assistance with daily living activities and may benefit from supported living arrangements or group homes.

- **Severe IDD:** People with severe IDD require significant support in all areas of life. They may have limited communication skills and depend on caregivers for most of their needs.

- **Profound IDD:** Individuals with profound IDD often have multiple disabilities and require constant care and supervision. Their communication abilities are very limited, and they may have significant physical limitations.

Beyond these categorical classifications, it is important to understand that each individual with IDD is unique, with their own strengths, challenges, and support needs. Person-centered planning approaches emphasize the importance of tailoring interventions and supports to meet the specific needs and goals of each individual, promoting autonomy, choice, and inclusion.

The neurological and genetic foundations of IDD provide insight into the biological factors that contribute to these conditions. Many cases of IDD have a genetic basis, resulting from chromosomal abnormalities, single-gene disorders, or complex genetic interactions. Down syndrome, for example, is caused by the presence of an extra copy of chromosome 21, leading to a characteristic set of physical and intellectual features. Fragile X syndrome, another common genetic cause of IDD, results from a mutation in the FMR1 gene on the X chromosome, affecting brain development and function.

Other genetic syndromes associated with IDD include Williams syndrome, Prader-Willi syndrome, and Rett syndrome. Each of these syndromes has distinct genetic causes and associated patterns of cognitive, behavioral, and physical characteristics. Genetic testing and counseling can help families understand the causes of IDD in their child and make informed decisions about reproductive planning and medical care.

In many cases, the causes of IDD are complex and multifactorial, involving interactions between genetic and environmental factors. Prenatal factors, such as maternal infections (e.g., rubella, cytomegalovirus), exposure to toxins (e.g., alcohol, drugs), and nutritional deficiencies, can increase the risk of IDD. Perinatal factors, such as premature birth, low birth weight, and birth injuries, can also contribute to developmental disabilities. Postnatal factors, such as infections (e.g., meningitis, encephalitis), traumatic brain injury, and exposure to toxins (e.g., lead), can also lead to IDD.

Neuroimaging studies, such as magnetic resonance imaging (MRI) and computed tomography (CT) scans, can provide valuable insight into brain structure and function in individuals with IDD. These studies have revealed that many individuals with IDD have abnormalities in brain size, shape, or connectivity, affecting cognitive and adaptive abilities.

Understanding the prevalence and demographic characteristics of IDD is important for informing public health policy and resource allocation. The prevalence of intellectual disability is estimated to be around 1% of the general population, with variations across different countries and regions. Developmental disabilities are more common, affecting an estimated 15% of children in the United States.

IDD affects individuals of all ages, races, ethnicities, and socioeconomic backgrounds. However, some groups are at higher risk for IDD than others. For example, children born to mothers who are young, have limited education, or experience poverty are at increased risk for developmental disabilities. Certain racial and ethnic minority groups also experience higher rates of IDD, potentially reflecting disparities in access to healthcare, education, and social services.

It is crucial to address these disparities and ensure that all individuals with IDD have access to the services and supports they need to thrive. Early intervention programs, such as early childhood education and therapy services, can improve developmental outcomes for young children with IDD. Access to quality healthcare, education, and vocational training can help individuals with IDD reach their fullest level of independence and lead meaningful lives.

Current research perspectives in the field of IDD emphasize individual potential and strengths, moving away from deficit-based models. Positive psychology and strengths-based approaches highlight the importance of focusing on what individuals with IDD can do, rather than what they cannot do. These approaches aim to empower individuals with IDD to develop their talents, pursue their interests, and achieve their goals.

Self-determination theory emphasizes the importance of autonomy, competence, and relatedness in promoting well-being and motivation. When individuals with IDD have opportunities to make choices, develop skills, and build meaningful relationships, they are more likely to experience a sense of purpose and satisfaction in life.

Assistive technology plays a vital role in supporting individuals with IDD to overcome barriers and participate more fully in society. Augmentative and alternative communication (AAC) devices can help individuals with limited speech to communicate their needs and desires. Adaptive equipment, such as wheelchairs, walkers, and modified utensils, can enhance mobility and independence.

In summary, the landscape of IDD is varied and complex, needing a multidisciplinary approach that incorporates clinical, biological, and social factors. By adopting a strengths-based perspective and tailoring interventions to meet the unique needs of each person, we can empower individuals with IDD to lead fulfilling lives and contribute to their communities. This requires ongoing efforts to promote inclusion, reduce stigma, and advocate for policies that support the rights and well-being of individuals with IDD and their families.

Learning Disabilities Impact Analysis

Learning disabilities affect how people take in, understand, remember, and use information. These differences in processing can show up in many ways and influence academic achievement, social skills, and everyday life.

One key area affected by learning disabilities is cognitive processing. This involves various mental operations such as attention, memory, language, and problem-solving. Difficulties in any of these areas can significantly impact learning. For instance, some individuals with learning disabilities may struggle with working memory, making it hard to hold information in mind while performing tasks like solving math problems or following multi-step instructions. Others may have problems with attention, leading to distractibility and difficulty focusing on tasks. These attention deficits aren't the same as Attention-Deficit/Hyperactivity

Disorder (ADHD), though they can sometimes co-occur. Instead, they represent a specific challenge within the broader scope of cognitive processing.

Auditory processing is another area where differences can emerge. Some individuals may have trouble distinguishing between similar sounds, which can affect reading and spelling. Visual processing deficits can also occur, leading to difficulties with tasks like recognizing letters or perceiving spatial relationships. These challenges highlight the complex interplay between perception and cognition in learning.

Sensory integration is the process by which we receive, organize, and interpret information from our senses. Difficulties with sensory integration can affect learning and behavior. Sensory integration dysfunction, sometimes called Sensory Processing Disorder (SPD), isn't recognized as a distinct disorder in the DSM-5 but is still a valid concept that occupational therapists use. People with SPD may be over- or under-sensitive to sensory input such as light, sound, touch, taste, or smell. For example, a child with tactile defensiveness may be uncomfortable with certain textures of clothing or may avoid messy activities. This discomfort can lead to anxiety and avoidance, which can interfere with learning and social interaction.

Vestibular processing, which involves the sense of balance and spatial orientation, can also be affected. Some individuals may have difficulty with activities that require balance and coordination, such as riding a bike or playing sports. Proprioceptive processing, which involves the sense of body position and movement, can also be affected. People with proprioceptive difficulties may have trouble with tasks that require fine motor skills, such as writing or buttoning a shirt.

Communication and comprehension are also frequently impacted. Language-based learning disabilities, such as dyslexia, can make it hard to decode words and understand written text. Dysgraphia can affect handwriting and spelling, while dyscalculia can make it hard to understand math concepts and perform calculations. These disabilities can affect not only academic performance but also self-esteem and social skills.

Individuals with autism spectrum disorder (ASD) may also experience communication and comprehension barriers. Some people with ASD may have difficulty understanding social cues, such as facial expressions and body language. They may also have trouble with pragmatic language skills, such as taking turns in conversation and understanding sarcasm. These difficulties can make it hard to form relationships and participate in social activities.

Neurological mechanisms play a vital role in learning, and differences in brain structure and function can contribute to learning disabilities. Neuroimaging studies have revealed that individuals with dyslexia, for example, may have differences in brain activation patterns during reading tasks. These differences can affect the efficiency and accuracy of reading.

Brain plasticity, the brain's ability to reorganize itself by forming new neural connections, offers hope for individuals with learning disabilities. Interventions that target specific cognitive skills can lead to changes in brain structure and function, improving learning outcomes.

Adaptive strategies and strengths-based approaches recognize that everyone learns differently and that individuals with learning disabilities have unique strengths and abilities. Rather than focusing solely on deficits, these approaches seek to identify and build upon individual strengths.

Assistive technology can also be a powerful tool for supporting learners with disabilities. Text-to-speech software can help individuals with dyslexia access written material, while speech-to-text software can help individuals with dysgraphia express their ideas in writing.

Case studies illustrate the complex interplay between learning disabilities and individual experiences.

Case Study 1: Alex, a student with dyslexia

Alex is an 8-year-old boy who struggles with reading. He has difficulty decoding words, even simple ones, and often misreads words or skips them altogether. His reading fluency is slow and labored, and he has trouble understanding what he reads.

Despite these challenges, Alex is a bright and curious child. He has a strong interest in science and enjoys conducting experiments. He is also a talented artist and loves to draw and paint.

With the support of his parents and teachers, Alex has been receiving specialized reading instruction. He is learning to use phonics strategies to decode words and is practicing reading aloud to improve his fluency. He also uses assistive technology, such as text-to-speech software, to access written material.

Alex's teachers have also identified his strengths and interests and are incorporating them into his learning activities. For example, they allow him to present his science projects in the form of drawings or models, rather than written reports. This allows him to demonstrate his understanding of the material without being limited by his reading difficulties.

Case Study 2: Maria, a student with sensory processing disorder

Maria is a 10-year-old girl who is highly sensitive to sensory input. She is easily overwhelmed by loud noises, bright lights, and strong smells. She also has difficulty with tactile input and avoids certain textures of clothing.

In the classroom, Maria is easily distracted by the noise and activity around her. She often covers her ears or hides under her desk to escape the sensory overload.

She also has difficulty with handwriting, as she finds the feeling of the pencil on the paper to be unpleasant.

Maria's parents have worked with an occupational therapist to develop strategies for managing her sensory sensitivities. They have created a sensory-friendly environment at home, with soft lighting, calming colors, and comfortable furniture. They also provide Maria with sensory tools, such as a weighted blanket and a fidget toy, to help her regulate her sensory input.

In the classroom, Maria's teacher has made accommodations to help her manage her sensory sensitivities. She allows Maria to sit in a quiet corner of the room, away from the noise and activity. She also provides Maria with noise-canceling headphones and a special pencil grip to make writing more comfortable.

These case studies highlight the importance of individualized assessment and intervention for students with learning disabilities. By understanding each student's unique strengths and challenges, educators can develop tailored strategies to support their learning and development.

It's vital to understand the social and emotional impact learning disabilities can have. Students may experience frustration, anxiety, and low self-esteem due to academic struggles. These emotional challenges can further interfere with learning and social interactions. Creating a supportive and inclusive classroom environment is essential for promoting the well-being of students with learning disabilities.

Teachers can foster a positive classroom climate by using strategies such as:

- Providing positive reinforcement and encouragement

- Celebrating successes and effort

- Teaching coping skills and stress management techniques

- Promoting peer support and collaboration

Parents and families also play a crucial role in supporting students with learning disabilities. Open communication between home and school is essential for ensuring that students receive consistent support and accommodations. Parents can also advocate for their children's needs and work with educators to develop individualized education programs (IEPs) that address their specific learning challenges.

Ultimately, understanding the impact of different disabilities on learning requires a shift in perspective. By recognizing the strengths and potential of every learner, and by providing appropriate support and accommodations, we can empower individuals with disabilities to achieve their goals and lead fulfilling lives. Instead of viewing learning disabilities as barriers, we can see them as differences that require understanding, acceptance, and innovative approaches to teaching and learning.

Personalized Learning Strategies

Creating individualized learning approaches for students with severe to profound disabilities requires a deep understanding of their unique strengths, needs, and preferences. The foundation of such approaches lies in carefully assessing each student's learning profile, adapting instructional methods, integrating assistive technology, and collaboratively setting goals. This file serves as a guide to these key components, offering practical strategies for implementing person-centered educational planning.

The cornerstone of personalized learning is a thorough assessment of each student's individual learning profile. This assessment goes beyond standardized tests and focuses on identifying specific strengths, challenges, and preferences. Educators should employ a variety of assessment methods, including observations, interviews with family members and caregivers, and formal evaluations, to gain a holistic understanding of the student's abilities.

Observations in different settings, such as the classroom, home, and community, can offer valuable insights into a student's learning style and preferences. For example, an educator might observe that a student responds positively to visual cues or tactile prompts. These observations can inform the design of instructional materials and activities.

Interviews with family members and caregivers are essential for gathering information about a student's history, interests, and communication style. Family members can provide information about the student's early development, medical history, and any previous interventions or therapies. They can also share insights into the student's likes, dislikes, and preferred ways of interacting with the world.

Formal evaluations, conducted by qualified professionals such as psychologists, therapists, and special educators, can provide valuable data about a student's cognitive, adaptive, and communication skills. These evaluations may include standardized tests, such as intelligence tests and adaptive behavior scales, as well as informal assessments designed to evaluate specific skills.

Once a student's learning profile has been assessed, educators can begin to customize instructional methods to meet their individual needs. This may involve modifying the curriculum, adapting teaching strategies, and creating individualized learning materials.

Curriculum modification involves adjusting the content and expectations of the general education curriculum to make it accessible to students with severe to profound disabilities. This may involve breaking down complex tasks into smaller, more manageable steps, simplifying language, and providing additional support and scaffolding. For example, a student who is learning to identify colors might begin by sorting objects by color, then move on to labeling colors, and finally to identifying colors in pictures.

Adapting teaching strategies involves using a variety of instructional techniques to engage students and promote learning. This may involve using visual aids, hands-on activities, and assistive technology. For example, a teacher might use picture cards to communicate instructions to a student who has limited verbal communication skills. They might also use manipulatives, such as blocks or beads, to teach math concepts.

Creating individualized learning materials involves designing materials that are tailored to a student's specific needs and preferences. This may involve creating adapted books, worksheets, and activities. For example, a teacher might create a social story to help a student understand a social situation, such as going to the doctor. They might also create a sensory bin filled with objects that are interesting and stimulating to the student.

Adaptive technology can play a crucial role in supporting students with severe to profound disabilities. This includes a wide range of devices and software that can help students access information, communicate, and participate in learning activities.

Assistive technology can help students with physical disabilities access computers and other devices. This may include alternative keyboards, switches, and eye-tracking systems. Alternative keyboards allow students to type using a variety of input methods, such as single switches or head pointers. Switches can be used to control a computer with a simple movement, such as a blink or a head turn. Eye-tracking systems allow students to control a computer using their eyes.

Communication devices can help students with limited verbal communication skills express themselves. This may include speech-generating devices, picture exchange systems, and sign language. Speech-generating devices allow students to communicate by selecting words or phrases from a menu. Picture exchange systems involve exchanging pictures to communicate needs and wants. Sign language is a visual language that uses hand gestures and facial expressions.

Software and apps can help students with cognitive disabilities learn academic skills. This may include programs that teach reading, math, and writing. These programs often use visual supports, audio prompts, and interactive activities to engage students and promote learning.

Collaborative goal-setting is an important part of the individualized learning process. It involves working with the student, family members, and other professionals to identify goals that are meaningful and achievable. These goals should be based on the student's strengths, needs, and interests, and they should be aligned with the student's overall educational plan.

Setting SMART goals (Specific, Measurable, Achievable, Relevant, Time-bound) provides a framework for ensuring that goals are realistic and attainable. Specific goals are clearly defined and focused. Measurable goals can be tracked and evaluated. Achievable goals are challenging but within the student's reach. Relevant goals are meaningful and important to the student. Time-bound goals have a clear deadline for completion.

Regular progress monitoring is essential for tracking a student's progress toward their goals. This involves collecting data on a regular basis and using it to make adjustments to the student's instructional program. Data can be collected through a variety of methods, such as observations, work samples, and assessments.

Adjusting goals and strategies based on progress monitoring data ensures that the student is making progress and that the instructional program is effective. If a student is not making progress toward a goal, the team may need to adjust the goal or the strategies being used to support the student.

Person-centered planning is a holistic approach to educational planning that focuses on the individual student and their unique needs, strengths, and aspirations. It involves working collaboratively with the student, family members, and other professionals to develop a plan that is tailored to the student's individual circumstances.

Focusing on strengths and abilities rather than deficits is a key principle of person-centered planning. This involves identifying the student's strengths and using them as a foundation for learning and growth. For example, a student who is good at drawing might use their artistic skills to express themselves or to learn academic concepts.

Incorporating student preferences and interests into educational planning increases engagement and motivation. This involves finding out what the student enjoys doing and incorporating those activities into the learning process. For example, a student who loves music might learn math concepts through playing musical instruments.

Promoting self-determination and choice empowers students to take control of their own learning. This involves giving students opportunities to make choices about their learning activities, goals, and strategies. For example, a student might choose which book to read or which assignment to complete.

Successful individualized learning interventions depend on understanding individual differences and embracing innovative teaching methods. Here are some examples:

Case Study 1: Enhancing Communication for a Student with Limited Verbal Skills

Sarah is a 12-year-old student with severe intellectual disability and limited verbal skills. She communicates primarily through gestures and facial expressions. To support Sarah's communication development, her team implemented a multi-faceted intervention plan. First, they introduced a speech-generating device (SGD) with personalized vocabulary and images. Sarah's family and therapists helped select images and words that reflected her daily routines, preferences, and needs. The team also taught Sarah's communication partners how to interpret her gestures and respond to her communication attempts. They used prompting strategies to encourage Sarah to use the SGD, starting with simple requests like "more" or "eat." Over time, Sarah learned to use the SGD to express a wider range of needs and preferences. Additionally, the team incorporated visual supports, such as picture schedules and social stories, to help Sarah understand routines and expectations. These interventions significantly enhanced Sarah's communication skills, allowing her to express herself more effectively and participate more fully in her daily activities.

Case Study 2: Promoting Independence in Daily Living Skills

Michael is a 16-year-old student with profound intellectual disability who requires assistance with many daily living skills. To promote Michael's independence, his team implemented a task analysis approach to teach him how to dress himself. They broke down the task of putting on a shirt into smaller, more manageable steps, such as "grab the shirt," "put your arm through the sleeve," and "pull the shirt down." The team used visual prompts, such as pictures and videos, to guide Michael through each step. They also provided physical prompts, such as hand-over-hand assistance, and gradually faded the prompts as Michael became more proficient. The team also worked with Michael's family to create a consistent routine at home, so that he could practice dressing himself every day. Over time, Michael learned to dress himself with minimal assistance, increasing his independence and self-esteem.

These case studies illustrate the importance of individualized assessment and intervention for students with severe to profound disabilities. By understanding each student's unique strengths and challenges, educators can develop tailored strategies to support their learning and development.

Effectively working with students who have severe to profound disabilities calls for a multidisciplinary team approach that brings together educators, therapists, family members, and other support staff. This collaboration ensures a comprehensive, well-coordinated plan that addresses all facets of the student's life.

Open communication and collaboration among team members are essential for ensuring that everyone is working towards the same goals. Regular team meetings can provide a forum for sharing information, discussing progress, and making adjustments to the student's plan. Communication tools, such as email, phone calls, and online platforms, can also facilitate communication between team members.

Shared decision-making respects the input and expertise of all team members, including the student and their family. This involves actively listening to each team member's perspective and incorporating their ideas into the student's plan. Shared decision-making promotes a sense of ownership and commitment among team members.

Consistent implementation across settings ensures that the student receives consistent support and instruction throughout the day. This involves coordinating activities and strategies across the classroom, home, and community. Consistent implementation can help the student generalize skills from one setting to another.

By prioritizing individualized learning approaches, educators can unlock the potential of students with severe to profound disabilities. This is achieved through a blend of careful assessment, adaptive instruction, assistive technology, and team collaboration, leading to meaningful advancements in each student's development and quality of life.

2

PLANNING INSTRUCTION AND LEARNING ENVIRONMENT

Crafting Personalized Learning Roadmaps

Crafting effective Individualized Education Programs, or IEPs, for students with severe to profound disabilities demands a meticulous and student-centered approach. These programs serve as personalized roadmaps, guiding educational teams in tailoring instruction and support to meet each student's unique needs and foster their growth. Understanding the legal framework and mastering the steps involved in IEP development are essential for educators dedicated to serving this population.

The foundation of any sound IEP lies in adherence to legal requirements. The Individuals with Disabilities Education Act, or IDEA, mandates that all students with disabilities receive a free and appropriate public education, or FAPE, in the least restrictive environment, or LRE. IDEA outlines specific procedures for IEP development, ensuring that students and their families are active participants in the process. Key components include comprehensive evaluations, measurable goals, and a statement of the special education and related services that the student will receive. States may have additional regulations, so educators must stay abreast of local guidelines to ensure compliance. Failing to meet these legal standards can have serious consequences, potentially leading to legal challenges and, more importantly, depriving students of their right to a quality education.

The IEP process begins with a thorough assessment of the student. This assessment should not merely focus on deficits; it must also identify the student's strengths, interests, and preferences. Understanding what motivates the student and what they excel at is key to creating a program that taps into their innate abilities and fosters a sense of accomplishment. Formal assessments, such as standardized tests, can provide valuable data on academic skills and cognitive functioning. However, these should be supplemented with informal assessments, such as observations, interviews with family members and caregivers, and analysis of student work samples. These qualitative methods offer a more holistic understanding of the student's learning style, communication abilities, and social-emotional development. Consider, for example, a student who struggles with verbal communication but demonstrates exceptional artistic talent. The IEP should incorporate opportunities for the student to express themselves through art, while also addressing their communication challenges through targeted interventions.

Once the assessment is complete, the next step is to translate the data into measurable and meaningful educational goals. IEP goals should be specific, measurable, achievable, relevant, and time-bound – often referred to as SMART goals. This ensures that progress can be objectively tracked and that the goals are aligned with the student's individual needs and the overall curriculum. Writing SMART goals for students with severe to profound disabilities requires creativity and a deep understanding of their abilities. Instead of focusing on abstract academic concepts, goals should be centered on functional skills that will enhance the student's independence and quality of life.

For instance, a goal might be: "By the end of the IEP year, the student will independently initiate a greeting to familiar adults in 4 out of 5 observed opportunities, using a verbal approximation, sign, or assistive technology device."

This goal is specific (initiating a greeting), measurable (4 out of 5 opportunities), achievable (realistic for the student's abilities), relevant (promoting social interaction), and time-bound (by the end of the IEP year). It's important to break down larger goals into smaller, more manageable steps, providing the student with frequent opportunities for success and reinforcement. Data collection is essential for monitoring progress toward IEP goals. Regular observations, task analyses, and data sheets can provide valuable information about the student's performance. The data should be analyzed regularly to determine whether the student is making adequate progress. If not, the IEP team should meet to revise the goals or instructional strategies.

Developing an effective IEP also requires the active participation of a multidisciplinary team. This team should include the student (when appropriate), parents or guardians, general education teachers, special education teachers, therapists (e.g., speech-language pathologists, occupational therapists, physical therapists), school psychologists, and other relevant professionals. Each member brings a unique perspective and expertise to the table, ensuring that the IEP addresses all aspects of the student's development. The parents' role is invaluable, as they possess the most intimate knowledge of their child's strengths, challenges, and preferences. They can provide insights into the student's home environment, family dynamics, and cultural background, all of which can influence the IEP. General education teachers play a crucial role in ensuring that the student has access to the general education curriculum, to the maximum extent appropriate. Special education teachers provide specialized instruction and support, adapting the curriculum to meet the student's individual needs. Therapists address specific skill deficits and provide interventions to improve the student's communication, motor skills, and sensory processing. The school psychologist can conduct assessments, provide counseling, and support the student's social-emotional well-being.

Collaboration and communication are essential for effective teamwork. Regular meetings, both formal and informal, should be held to discuss the student's progress, share ideas, and address any concerns. All team members should have access to the student's IEP and be familiar with their roles and responsibilities. Clear communication channels should be established to ensure that everyone is on the same page.

Beyond setting goals, the IEP must outline the specific special education and related services that the student will receive. This includes the type and frequency of instruction, therapies, and other supports. The IEP should also specify any accommodations or modifications that will be provided to ensure that the student can access the general education curriculum and participate in school activities. Accommodations are changes to how the student learns, while modifications are changes to what the student learns. For example, a student who has difficulty writing might be provided with the accommodation of using a keyboard. A student who is not able to master the same content as their peers might be provided with modified assignments that are tailored to their individual level. The IEP should also address the student's assistive technology needs. Assistive technology can range from low-tech devices, such as pencil grips and adapted utensils, to high-tech devices, such as communication devices and computer software. The IEP team should work together to identify the assistive technology that will best support the student's learning and independence.

Once the IEP is developed, it must be implemented with fidelity. This means that all team members must follow the IEP as written and provide the student with the services and supports that are outlined in the document. Regular monitoring of the student's progress is essential to ensure that the IEP is effective. Data should be collected regularly and analyzed to determine whether the student is making adequate progress toward their goals. If not, the IEP team should meet to revise the IEP and make any necessary changes. The IEP is not a static document; it should be reviewed and revised at least annually, or more frequently if needed.

The IEP team should meet regularly to discuss the student's progress and make any necessary adjustments to the IEP. The annual review provides an opportunity to reflect on the student's progress over the past year and to set new goals for the coming year.

Creating a supportive and inclusive learning environment is essential for students with severe to profound disabilities. This includes providing the student with opportunities to interact with their peers, both with and without disabilities. Inclusion can take many forms, from participating in general education classes to attending school-wide events. The goal of inclusion is to ensure that students with disabilities are fully integrated into the school community and have the same opportunities as their peers. It's also vital to consider the physical environment. Classrooms should be accessible, well-organized, and free from distractions. Sensory considerations are also important. Some students with severe to profound disabilities may be sensitive to certain stimuli, such as loud noises or bright lights. The classroom should be designed to minimize these stimuli and provide the student with a calming and supportive environment.

In addition to academic and functional skills, the IEP should also address the student's social-emotional development. Students with severe to profound disabilities may experience social isolation, anxiety, and depression. The IEP should include strategies to promote the student's social skills, self-esteem, and emotional well-being. This might involve providing opportunities for social interaction, teaching social skills, and providing counseling or therapy.

Finally, the IEP should address the student's transition to adulthood. Transition planning should begin in early adolescence and should focus on preparing the student for life after school. This includes helping the student develop the skills and knowledge they will need to live independently, work, and participate in their community. Transition services might include vocational training, job coaching, and independent living skills training. The IEP team should work with the student and their family to develop a transition plan that is tailored to their individual needs and goals.

In conclusion, developing effective IEPs for students with severe to profound disabilities requires a deep understanding of the legal requirements, a thorough assessment of the student's strengths and needs, measurable and meaningful goals, a collaborative team approach, and a commitment to providing the student with the supports and services they need to succeed. By embracing a holistic, student-centered approach, educators can empower these students to reach their full potential and lead fulfilling lives. The journey is not without its challenges, but the rewards of witnessing a student's growth and progress make it all worthwhile.

Specialized Teaching Approaches

Providing effective instruction to students with severe to profound disabilities often requires adapting or completely reimagining conventional teaching methods. These students need learning experiences crafted around their unique sensory, communication, and physical needs. This file examines particular teaching approaches with proven effectiveness.

One area of focus is adaptive communication. Many students with severe to profound disabilities have significant difficulties with traditional forms of communication. Adaptive communication techniques help these students express their wants, needs, and ideas in ways that are accessible to them. This includes augmentative and alternative communication (AAC) systems, which can range from simple picture boards to sophisticated speech-generating devices.

Picture Exchange Communication System (PECS) is one such method. PECS uses picture symbols to teach functional communication. Students learn to exchange a picture of a desired item or activity with a communication partner, who then provides the item or facilitates the activity. PECS promotes independence and initiation of communication, rather than simply responding to prompts. The system progresses through phases, teaching students to discriminate between pictures, construct simple sentences, and answer questions.

Sign language is another adaptive communication tool. While not all students with severe to profound disabilities can master complex sign language, many can learn basic signs to express common needs and wants. Using sign language alongside spoken words can also support understanding and language development. For students with visual impairments, tactile sign language, which involves molding the hands into the shapes of signs, can be effective.

Beyond these established methods, creating individualized communication systems is often necessary. This might involve using a combination of gestures, vocalizations, and tangible objects to represent different concepts. It is important to observe the student closely and identify any consistent patterns in their behavior that could be used as a basis for communication. For example, a student might consistently reach for a particular object when they want to use it. This could be interpreted as a request for that object and incorporated into their communication system.

Sensory integration is another vital area of instruction. Many students with severe to profound disabilities have sensory processing difficulties, which can affect their ability to learn and interact with the world. Sensory integration therapy aims to help students regulate their sensory input and respond to it in a more adaptive way. This can involve providing opportunities for sensory stimulation in a controlled and therapeutic environment.

Multi-sensory environments, often called "Snoezelen" rooms, are designed to provide a range of sensory experiences. These rooms typically include features such as soft lighting, calming music, tactile surfaces, and aromatherapy. The goal is to create a relaxing and stimulating environment that helps students to regulate their sensory input and reduce anxiety. Teachers need to learn how to utilize those sensory integration rooms to make them helpful for the student.

In the classroom, sensory integration strategies can be incorporated into daily routines. For example, providing students with opportunities to engage in proprioceptive activities, such as lifting heavy objects or pushing against a wall, can help them to regulate their arousal level and improve their focus. Tactile activities, such as playing with sand or water, can be calming and can also promote exploration and learning. Students with auditory sensitivities may benefit from wearing noise-canceling headphones or working in a quiet area of the classroom.

Assistive technology (AT) opens up possibilities for students with severe to profound disabilities. AT encompasses a wide range of devices and tools that can help students overcome barriers to learning and participation. Low-tech AT might include adapted writing utensils, picture cards, and modified seating. High-tech AT includes speech-generating devices, adaptive computer software, and environmental control systems.

When selecting assistive technology, it's important to consider the student's individual needs, abilities, and preferences. An occupational therapist or assistive technology specialist can conduct a thorough assessment to identify the most appropriate tools. Funding for assistive technology can be a challenge, but there are a number of resources available, including state and federal programs, private foundations, and fundraising initiatives.

Switch-activated devices are a powerful form of AT for students with limited motor control. A switch can be activated by a variety of movements, such as pressing with a hand, foot, or head. Once activated, the switch can be used to control a variety of devices, such as toys, appliances, and computers. This allows students to participate in activities that would otherwise be inaccessible to them.

Students who cannot use their hands may be able to use head switches to control a computer or other device.

Differentiated learning methodologies acknowledge that students learn in different ways and at different paces. For students with severe to profound disabilities, differentiation is not just a matter of modifying assignments or providing extra support; it requires a fundamental rethinking of the curriculum and instructional methods. This includes breaking down complex tasks into smaller, more manageable steps, providing ample opportunities for practice and reinforcement, and using a variety of instructional strategies to appeal to different learning styles.

Task analysis is a technique for breaking down complex tasks into smaller, more manageable steps. This involves identifying all of the individual steps required to complete a task and then teaching each step in a systematic way. Task analysis is particularly useful for teaching functional skills, such as dressing, eating, and toileting. For example, the task of washing hands can be broken down into the following steps: turn on the water, wet hands, apply soap, rub hands together, rinse hands, dry hands, turn off the water. Each step can then be taught individually, with the student receiving reinforcement for each step completed successfully.

Scaffolding is a technique for providing temporary support to students as they learn new skills. This might involve providing verbal prompts, physical assistance, or visual cues. As the student becomes more proficient, the scaffolding is gradually removed until the student can perform the task independently. Scaffolding should be tailored to the student's individual needs and abilities. For example, a student who is learning to dress themselves might initially need help with buttoning their shirt. As they become more proficient, the teacher can gradually reduce the amount of assistance they provide until the student can button their shirt independently.

Creating multi-sensory learning experiences involves engaging multiple senses simultaneously. This can help students to better understand and retain information. For example, when teaching about different types of fruits, the teacher might provide students with opportunities to see, touch, smell, and taste the fruits. They might also listen to songs or stories about fruits, or create artwork inspired by fruits. This multi-sensory approach can make learning more engaging and meaningful for students with severe to profound disabilities.

Innovative approaches continue to emerge in the field of special education. One example is the use of virtual reality (VR) to create immersive learning experiences. VR can provide students with opportunities to explore environments and engage in activities that would otherwise be inaccessible to them. For example, a student who is unable to travel might use VR to visit a museum or a foreign country. VR can also be used to simulate real-life situations, such as crossing the street or ordering food at a restaurant.

Another trend is the use of robotics to support students with severe to profound disabilities. Robots can be used to provide physical assistance, such as helping students to stand or walk. They can also be used to provide social interaction and companionship. Some robots are designed to be interactive and responsive, providing students with opportunities to practice social skills and engage in meaningful conversations.

Ultimately, the most effective teaching approaches are those that are tailored to the individual needs and strengths of each student. It is important to be flexible, creative, and willing to try new things. By working collaboratively with families, therapists, and other professionals, educators can create learning experiences that maximize student potential and promote independence, engagement, and a higher quality of life. Continual assessment and data collection are key to monitoring student progress and adjusting instructional strategies as needed. What new technologies and approaches will further transform special education in the years to come?

Designing Inclusive Learning Spaces

Designing effective learning spaces for students with severe to profound disabilities means carefully considering the physical environment and its impact on their ability to learn and thrive. This involves modifying the classroom to be more accessible, sensory-friendly, and safe, fostering independence, comfort, and optimal learning.

One of the primary considerations is adapting the physical space. This goes beyond simply meeting basic accessibility standards; it requires a thoughtful approach to furniture selection, layout, and overall organization.

Ergonomic furniture is essential for promoting comfort and proper posture, which can significantly affect a student's ability to focus and participate in activities. Adjustable-height tables and chairs allow for customization to meet individual needs, accommodating students who use wheelchairs or have other physical limitations. Seating options should include a variety of choices, such as beanbag chairs, rocking chairs, or floor cushions, to provide alternative positions and address sensory preferences. Consider the fabric of the furniture as well; smooth, easily cleanable surfaces are ideal for hygiene and minimizing distractions.

The arrangement of furniture should promote clear pathways and minimize clutter. Wide aisles are crucial for students using wheelchairs, walkers, or other mobility devices. Consider creating distinct learning zones within the classroom, each designed for specific activities. For instance, a quiet reading area with comfortable seating and soft lighting can provide a calming space for students who need to de-stress. A more active learning area with adaptable tables and manipulatives can encourage participation in hands-on activities.

Sensory regulation zones are a vital component of an inclusive classroom for students with severe to profound disabilities. These zones provide a designated space where students can manage their sensory input and regulate their emotional state. The design of these zones should be based on the individual needs and preferences of the students in the classroom.

A sensory regulation zone might include a variety of sensory tools, such as weighted blankets, textured balls, and visual aids like calming light displays. These tools can help students to self-soothe and regulate their sensory input. A quiet, enclosed space, such as a small tent or a partitioned area, can provide a sense of security and reduce distractions. Soft lighting, neutral colors, and minimal visual clutter can also contribute to a calming atmosphere.

The sensory regulation zone should be easily accessible to all students and should be incorporated into the daily routine. Students should be taught how to use the zone and its resources effectively, and should be encouraged to use it whenever they feel overwhelmed or dysregulated. Regular monitoring and evaluation of the zone's effectiveness can help to ensure that it continues to meet the needs of the students in the classroom.

Adaptive equipment plays a pivotal role in supporting students with severe to profound disabilities, enabling them to participate more fully in classroom activities and enhance their independence. Proper placement of this equipment is crucial for maximizing its effectiveness and ensuring student safety.

Wheelchairs and walkers should be positioned in a way that allows for easy access to learning materials and activities. Ramps or lifts may be necessary to navigate changes in floor level. Communication devices, such as speech-generating devices or communication boards, should be readily available and positioned for optimal use. Consider using mounting systems that allow for flexible positioning and adjustment.

Positioning devices, such as standers or specialized seating systems, should be used to promote proper posture and alignment. These devices can also help to improve circulation, reduce fatigue, and prevent contractures. Ensure that all adaptive equipment is properly fitted and adjusted to meet the individual needs of each student. Regular maintenance and inspection of adaptive equipment are essential for ensuring its safety and functionality.

Creating a sensory-friendly environment is paramount for students with severe to profound disabilities, as they are often highly sensitive to sensory input. Managing the visual and auditory environment is key to minimizing distractions and promoting a sense of calm and well-being.

Visual clutter should be kept to a minimum. Use neutral colors and avoid busy patterns on walls and floors. Organize materials and supplies in labeled containers to reduce visual chaos. Consider using room dividers or screens to create smaller, more defined spaces.

Lighting should be soft and diffused, avoiding harsh fluorescent lights. Natural light is ideal, but if that's not possible, use full-spectrum lighting or adjustable lamps to control the intensity and color of the light. Provide window coverings, such as blinds or curtains, to block out excessive sunlight or glare.

Noise levels should be carefully managed. Use sound-absorbing materials, such as acoustic panels, carpets, and drapes, to reduce reverberation and background noise. Provide noise-canceling headphones for students who are particularly sensitive to sound. Establish clear expectations for noise levels during different activities.

In addition to visual and auditory considerations, it's important to manage other sensory inputs, such as smells and textures. Avoid using strong perfumes or scented products. Provide a variety of tactile materials for students to explore, such as soft fabrics, textured toys, and sensory bins filled with rice, beans, or water beads.

Accessibility is a core principle of inclusive classroom design. This involves ensuring that all students can access and participate in all aspects of the learning environment, regardless of their physical, sensory, or cognitive abilities.

This includes providing accessible entrances and exits, ramps or lifts for changes in floor level, and accessible restrooms. Signage should be clear, concise, and easy to read, using large print and tactile elements.

Learning materials should be available in a variety of formats, such as Braille, large print, audio, and digital. Provide assistive technology, such as screen readers, voice recognition software, and alternative keyboards, to support students with disabilities.

Classroom activities should be designed to be inclusive and adaptable, allowing all students to participate at their own level. Provide opportunities for choice and self-direction. Use differentiated instruction strategies to meet the diverse learning needs of students.

Safety and comfort are paramount considerations in designing inclusive learning spaces for students with severe to profound disabilities. Creating a safe and comfortable environment can help students to feel secure, reduce anxiety, and promote optimal learning.

This includes implementing safety protocols, such as emergency evacuation plans and procedures for managing medical emergencies. Ensure that all staff members are trained in basic first aid and CPR.

The classroom should be free of hazards, such as sharp objects, loose wires, and slippery floors. Furniture should be stable and secure, and all equipment should be properly maintained.

Temperature and ventilation should be carefully controlled to ensure a comfortable environment. Provide access to fresh air and natural light whenever possible.

Personal space should be respected and protected. Provide individual workstations or designated areas where students can retreat for privacy.

Creating a positive and supportive classroom culture is essential for promoting safety and comfort. Encourage empathy, respect, and acceptance among all students. Provide opportunities for social interaction and collaboration.

Ultimately, the goal of designing inclusive learning spaces is to create an environment that promotes independence, comfort, and learning potential for all students. This requires a comprehensive and individualized approach, taking into account the unique needs and abilities of each student.

By carefully considering the physical space, sensory environment, accessibility, and safety, educators can create classrooms that empower students with severe to profound disabilities to thrive. This involves a commitment to ongoing assessment, reflection, and adaptation, as well as collaboration with families, therapists, and other professionals. The evolution of technology and educational approaches will continue to shape the future of inclusive classroom design, creating even more opportunities for students with disabilities to reach their full potential. How can technology be seamlessly integrated to enhance environmental control and personalized learning experiences within these spaces?

Positive Behavior Support Systems

Positive Behavior Support Systems are essential for fostering a safe, predictable, and positive learning environment for students with severe to profound disabilities. These systems emphasize understanding the reasons behind challenging behaviors and creating individualized strategies that promote skill development and emotional well-being.

Functional Behavior Assessment (FBA) serves as the cornerstone of effective behavior support. Rather than simply reacting to challenging behaviors, FBA seeks to understand the purpose, or function, the behavior serves for the student. This involves gathering information through observations, interviews with caregivers and staff, and review of existing records. The goal is to identify the specific events, situations, or conditions that trigger the behavior (antecedents) and the consequences that maintain it (reinforcers). For example, a student might engage in self-injurious behavior (SIB) to escape a demanding task, gain attention from a caregiver, or experience a particular sensory input.

To conduct an effective FBA, educators should begin by clearly defining the target behavior in observable and measurable terms. Instead of saying "the student is disruptive," a more precise description would be "the student yells and throws objects when presented with a math worksheet." This allows for more objective data collection and tracking of progress.

Next, identify the antecedents, or triggers, that precede the behavior. This may involve analyzing the time of day, activity, setting, or individuals present when the behavior occurs. Keeping an ABC (Antecedent-Behavior-Consequence) data log can be a useful tool for this purpose. For instance, the log might reveal that the student's yelling and throwing behavior consistently occurs when presented with a math worksheet (antecedent), they yell and throw the worksheet (behavior), and the teacher removes the worksheet (consequence).

The final step of the FBA is to determine the function of the behavior. In other words, what does the student gain or avoid by engaging in the behavior? Common functions include:

- **Attention:** The student engages in the behavior to gain attention from peers or adults.

- **Escape/Avoidance:** The student engages in the behavior to escape or avoid a task, activity, or situation.

- **Sensory Stimulation:** The student engages in the behavior to obtain sensory input, such as tactile, visual, or auditory stimulation.

- **Tangible Reinforcement:** The student engages in the behavior to obtain a desired object or activity.

Once the function of the behavior has been identified, the team can develop a Behavior Intervention Plan (BIP) that addresses the underlying need and teaches the student more appropriate ways to meet that need.

Proactive behavior management strategies form the foundation of a positive and supportive classroom environment. These strategies focus on preventing challenging behaviors from occurring in the first place by creating a predictable, structured, and engaging learning environment.

One key element of proactive behavior management is establishing clear expectations and routines. Students with severe to profound disabilities benefit from knowing what is expected of them and what will happen next. Visual schedules, social stories, and consistent routines can help to provide this predictability. For example, a visual schedule might depict the sequence of activities for the day, such as arrival, circle time, snack, and individual work.

Another important strategy is to create a positive and supportive classroom climate. This involves building positive relationships with students, providing frequent praise and encouragement, and focusing on their strengths and accomplishments. Educators can use positive reinforcement to motivate students to engage in desired behaviors. This might involve providing verbal praise, tangible rewards, or access to preferred activities when the student demonstrates appropriate behavior. For example, a student who remains seated and attentive during circle time might be rewarded with a sticker or a few minutes of playtime with a favorite toy.

Modifying the environment can also help to prevent challenging behaviors. This might involve reducing distractions, providing sensory supports, or adapting tasks to make them more manageable. For instance, a student who is easily over-stimulated by noise might benefit from sitting in a quiet corner of the classroom or wearing noise-canceling headphones.

De-escalation methods are essential for managing challenging behaviors that do occur, despite proactive strategies. The goal of de-escalation is to safely and re-spectfully help the student regain control and return to a calm state.

When a student begins to exhibit signs of agitation or distress, it is important to remain calm and avoid escalating the situation. Speak in a calm, quiet voice and use simple, clear language. Give the student space and avoid making sudden movements or gestures.

Offer the student choices whenever possible. This can help them to feel more in control and reduce their sense of powerlessness. For example, you might ask, "Would you like to take a break in the quiet area, or would you like to talk about what's bothering you?"

If the student is engaging in disruptive behavior, it is important to set clear and consistent limits. State the expectation in a calm and respectful manner, and explain the consequences of not following the expectation. For example, you might say, "I understand you're upset, but it's not okay to throw toys. If you throw another toy, you will need to take a break from playing with toys for a few minutes."

In some cases, physical intervention may be necessary to ensure the safety of the student and others. However, physical intervention should only be used as a last resort, and only by staff who have been properly trained in safe and effective techniques.

Positive reinforcement systems are a crucial component of behavior support. These systems focus on rewarding desired behaviors rather than punishing undesired behaviors. This approach is more effective in promoting long-term behavior change and creating a positive learning environment.

The key to an effective positive reinforcement system is to identify the reinforcers that are most motivating for each student. This may involve observing the student, asking their caregivers, or conducting a reinforcer assessment. Common reinforcers include verbal praise, tangible rewards, access to preferred activities, and social recognition.

Reinforcers should be delivered immediately and consistently when the student engages in the desired behavior. This helps the student to make the connection between the behavior and the reward. As the student becomes more consistent with the desired behavior, the reinforcement schedule can be gradually faded.

Token economy systems can be an effective way to implement positive reinforcement in the classroom. In a token economy, students earn tokens for engaging in desired behaviors. These tokens can then be exchanged for a variety of reinforcers, such as toys, games, or special privileges.

The successful implementation of Positive Behavior Support Systems hinges on a deep understanding of the individual student's needs, strengths, and preferences. This requires ongoing communication and collaboration among educators, caregivers, therapists, and other professionals.

Identifying behavior triggers is crucial for preventing challenging behaviors before they occur. This involves carefully analyzing the antecedents, or events that precede the behavior. By understanding what triggers the behavior, educators can modify the environment, provide proactive supports, and teach the student alternative coping strategies.

Creating individualized behavior intervention plans is essential for addressing the unique needs of each student. The BIP should be based on the results of the FBA and should outline specific strategies for preventing challenging behaviors, teaching replacement behaviors, and responding to challenging behaviors when they do occur. The BIP should be a collaborative effort, involving the student, their caregivers, and other members of the educational team.

Training staff in supportive interaction techniques is essential for ensuring that all staff members are equipped to effectively support students with challenging behaviors. This training should cover topics such as active listening, de-escalation strategies, and positive reinforcement techniques. Staff members should also be trained in how to implement the student's BIP and how to collect data on their progress.

Implementing consistent compassionate management approaches is crucial for creating a predictable and supportive learning environment. This involves setting clear expectations, providing consistent consequences for inappropriate behavior, and responding to students with empathy and understanding. It is important to remember that challenging behaviors are often a form of communication, and that students may be struggling to express their needs in more appropriate ways.

A key component of effective behavior support is understanding the underlying communication and emotional needs of the student. Students with severe to profound disabilities may have difficulty expressing their needs verbally, and their challenging behaviors may be a way of communicating their frustration, anxiety, or discomfort. By carefully observing the student and listening to their nonverbal cues, educators can gain insight into their underlying needs and provide appropriate support. This could involve teaching the student alternative communication methods, such as sign language or picture exchange, or providing sensory supports to help them regulate their emotions.

In conclusion, Positive Behavior Support Systems are essential for creating a positive and supportive learning environment for students with severe to profound disabilities. By understanding the reasons behind challenging behaviors and implementing individualized strategies that promote skill development and emotional well-being, educators can help these students to reach their full potential. These strategies are not about control, but rather about creating environments where students feel safe, understood, and empowered to learn and grow. The focus remains on proactively supporting communication, emotional regulation, and skill acquisition.

3

ASSESSMENT IN SPECIAL EDUCATION

Assessment Foundations in Special Education

Assessment in special education is a cornerstone of effective instruction, as it informs educators about a student's strengths, needs, and progress. Different types of assessments serve distinct purposes, each contributing valuable information to the educational process. Diagnostic assessments pinpoint specific learning challenges, formative assessments provide ongoing feedback to adjust instruction, and summative assessments evaluate overall learning outcomes. The landscape of assessment shifts significantly when considering students with severe to profound disabilities.

Diagnostic assessments are used to identify specific areas of difficulty and determine the underlying causes of learning challenges. For typically developing students, these assessments might involve standardized tests that compare their performance to that of their peers. However, for students with severe to profound disabilities, standardized tests are often inappropriate and yield little useful information. Instead, diagnostic assessments for these students rely heavily on observations, interviews with caregivers, and informal assessments that examine specific skills in functional contexts. For instance, a diagnostic assessment might involve observing a student during mealtime to identify difficulties with chewing, swallowing, or self-feeding, or assessing their ability to follow simple directions during a daily routine.

Formative assessments are ongoing evaluations that provide continuous feedback on student learning and guide instructional decisions. In general education classrooms, formative assessments might include quizzes, class discussions, or quick writing assignments. For students with severe to profound disabilities, formative assessment takes on an even more individualized and adaptive approach. It involves closely monitoring a student's responses to instruction and making adjustments based on their performance. This might involve tracking the number of times a student successfully completes a task with assistance, noting their level of engagement during an activity, or observing their interactions with peers and adults. For example, if a student is learning to use a switch to activate a toy, the teacher might track the number of times the student independently activates the switch and adjust the placement of the switch or the type of toy to maximize their success.

Summative assessments are used to evaluate a student's overall learning and mastery of specific skills or content at the end of a unit, semester, or school year. In general education, summative assessments typically involve standardized tests, final exams, or major projects. However, these types of assessments are often not suitable for students with severe to profound disabilities. Instead, summative assessments for these students focus on evaluating their progress toward individualized goals and objectives outlined in their Individualized Education Program (IEP). This might involve demonstrating mastery of functional skills, such as dressing, grooming, or preparing a simple meal, or demonstrating the ability to communicate basic needs and preferences. The assessment might be a portfolio showcasing work samples, photographs, and videos demonstrating the student's progress over time.

Evaluating students with significant learning differences presents unique challenges that require educators to adapt their assessment strategies. Traditional assessment methods often rely on standardized procedures, written responses, and verbal communication, which can be inaccessible to students with severe disabilities. For instance, a student with limited communication skills may not be able to express their understanding of a concept through writing or speech. Similarly, a student with motor impairments may struggle to manipulate materials or complete tasks within a specified time frame.

One challenge lies in differentiating between a student's lack of knowledge or skill and their inability to demonstrate what they know due to physical or communication limitations. It's essential to use a variety of assessment methods that allow students to demonstrate their abilities in different ways. This might involve using assistive technology, such as communication devices or adapted switches, to enable students to express themselves or complete tasks. It might also involve modifying the format of assessment tasks to make them more accessible, such as using visual supports, simplified instructions, or hands-on activities.

Another challenge is ensuring that assessments are aligned with the student's individualized goals and objectives. Students with severe to profound disabilities often have IEPs that focus on developing functional skills, communication skills, and social-emotional skills. Therefore, assessments should be designed to measure progress in these areas, rather than focusing solely on academic content. This requires educators to work closely with the student's IEP team to develop assessment methods that are both meaningful and relevant to the student's individual needs.

Individualized and adaptive assessment strategies are paramount when evaluating students with severe to profound disabilities. These strategies recognize that each student has unique strengths, needs, and learning styles, and that assessments should be tailored to accommodate these differences. Individualized assessment involves developing assessment methods that are specifically designed for the student, taking into account their individual abilities, preferences, and challenges. This might involve modifying existing assessment tools or creating new ones that are more appropriate for the student.

Adaptive assessment involves adjusting the assessment process based on the student's responses and performance. This might involve providing additional support or prompts, modifying the task demands, or allowing the student to use assistive technology. Adaptive assessment ensures that the student is given every opportunity to demonstrate their abilities and that the assessment accurately reflects their knowledge and skills.

One example of an individualized and adaptive assessment strategy is the use of task analysis. Task analysis involves breaking down a complex task into smaller, more manageable steps, and then assessing the student's ability to complete each step. This allows educators to identify specific areas where the student needs support and to provide targeted instruction to help them master the task. For example, if a student is learning to brush their teeth, the task might be broken down into the following steps: (1) pick up the toothbrush, (2) apply toothpaste, (3) wet the toothbrush, (4) brush the top teeth, (5) brush the bottom teeth, (6) rinse the toothbrush, and (7) put the toothbrush away. The educator would then observe the student as they attempt to complete each step and provide assistance as needed.

Another example is the use of portfolio assessment. Portfolio assessment involves collecting samples of a student's work over time to document their progress and achievements. This might include photographs, videos, artwork, writing samples, or other artifacts that demonstrate the student's learning. Portfolio assessment provides a holistic view of the student's abilities and allows them to showcase their strengths and accomplishments. It also provides valuable information for IEP planning and program evaluation.

Traditional assessment methods often need modification for students with severe disabilities to ensure they are accessible, meaningful, and accurately reflect the student's abilities. This might involve adapting the format of the assessment, providing accommodations, or using alternative assessment methods.

One common modification is to simplify the language and instructions used in the assessment. Students with cognitive impairments may struggle to understand complex language or abstract concepts. Therefore, it's important to use clear, concise language and to provide visual supports to help them understand the task. For example, instead of asking a student to "identify the object that is used for eating," the educator might show the student a picture of a spoon and ask them to "point to the spoon."

Another modification is to provide accommodations to help students overcome physical or sensory limitations. This might involve providing assistive technology, such as a communication device or a adapted switch, or modifying the physical environment to make it more accessible. For example, a student with motor impairments might use a head pointer to indicate their responses, or a student with visual impairments might use a tactile version of the assessment.

Alternative assessment methods can be used to evaluate skills and knowledge in ways that are more appropriate for students with severe disabilities. This might involve using performance-based assessments, where students demonstrate their skills through hands-on activities, or using observations to document a student's progress in natural settings. For example, instead of giving a student a written test on their knowledge of hygiene skills, the educator might observe the student as they wash their hands or brush their teeth.

Ethical considerations are paramount in the assessment of students with severe to profound disabilities. Educators must ensure that assessments are fair, equitable, and do not discriminate against students based on their disability. This involves using assessment methods that are appropriate for the student's individual needs and abilities, providing accommodations to ensure they have equal access to the assessment, and interpreting the results in a way that is sensitive to their unique circumstances. It is also important to obtain informed consent from parents or guardians before conducting any assessments and to protect the student's privacy and confidentiality.

Comprehensive Disability-Specific Evaluation Methods

When assessing students with severe to profound disabilities, educators need specialized methods that go beyond typical tests. These methods should address the unique challenges and strengths of each student.

Specialized Assessment Protocols for Various Disability Categories

Different disabilities require different assessment approaches. For students with intellectual disabilities, assessments focus on adaptive behavior and cognitive skills. For those with sensory impairments, evaluations must consider their specific sensory needs. And for individuals with multiple disabilities, assessments should cover all areas of impact.

- **Intellectual Disability:** Assessing intellectual disability involves looking at both intellectual functioning and adaptive behavior. Intellectual functioning refers to a person's ability to learn, reason, solve problems, and understand concepts. Adaptive behavior includes everyday social and practical skills. These skills are essential for independent living. Standardized tests, like the Vineland Adaptive Behavior Scales, help measure adaptive behavior. These scales assess areas such as communication, daily living skills, socialization, and motor skills. Observational assessments are also very useful. Educators can observe a student's ability to perform daily tasks, interact with others, and follow instructions.

- **Sensory Impairments:** Students with visual impairments need assessments that don't rely heavily on sight. Tactile assessments, which use touch, are helpful. For instance, a student might identify objects by feeling their shape and texture. Auditory assessments can evaluate a student's ability to hear and process sounds. This might involve identifying different sounds or following spoken directions. Orientation and mobility assessments are crucial for students with visual impairments. These assessments evaluate a student's ability to move around safely and independently.

- **Multiple Disabilities:** Assessing students with multiple disabilities requires a team approach. This team might include special educators, therapists, and medical professionals. Each member brings their expertise to the assessment process. Assessments should cover all areas affected by the disabilities. This includes cognitive, physical, sensory, and communication skills. It's vital to prioritize the most pressing needs and develop goals that address these needs.

Multi-Dimensional Evaluation Approaches

A multi-dimensional evaluation looks at all aspects of a student's life. This includes their physical, cognitive, social, and emotional development. It also considers their environment, including home, school, and community.

- **Physical Development:** Assessing physical development involves looking at motor skills, sensory abilities, and overall health. Motor skills include both gross motor skills (like walking and running) and fine motor skills (like grasping and manipulating objects). Sensory abilities include vision, hearing, touch, taste, and smell. Health assessments might involve reviewing medical records or conducting physical examinations.

- **Cognitive Development:** Cognitive assessments evaluate a student's ability to think, learn, and solve problems. These assessments might involve observing a student's problem-solving strategies, assessing their memory and attention skills, or evaluating their understanding of concepts.

- **Social and Emotional Development:** Assessing social and emotional development involves looking at a student's ability to interact with others, manage their emotions, and form relationships. This might involve observing a student's interactions with peers and adults, assessing their ability to express their feelings, or evaluating their self-esteem and self-confidence.

- **Environmental Factors:** A student's environment can greatly affect their development and learning. Assessments should consider factors such as the student's home life, school environment, and community resources. This might involve interviewing parents or caregivers, observing the student in different settings, or evaluating the accessibility of the school and community.

Sensory and Cognitive Assessment Techniques

Sensory and cognitive assessments help educators understand how a student processes information. These assessments identify any sensory or cognitive impairments that might affect learning.

- **Sensory Assessments:** Sensory assessments evaluate a student's ability to process sensory information. This includes vision, hearing, touch, taste, smell, and proprioception (body awareness). Sensory Processing Measures can help identify sensory processing difficulties. These measures involve observing a student's responses to different sensory stimuli.

- **Cognitive Assessments:** Cognitive assessments evaluate a student's intellectual functioning and cognitive abilities. This might involve using standardized tests, such as the Bayley Scales of Infant and Toddler Development, or conducting informal assessments. Informal assessments might include observing a student's problem-solving strategies, assessing their memory and attention skills, or evaluating their understanding of concepts.

Communication-Based Assessment Strategies

Communication is key to learning and development. Communication-based assessments evaluate a student's ability to express themselves and understand others.

- **Expressive Communication:** Expressive communication refers to a person's ability to communicate their thoughts, feelings, and needs to others. This might involve using verbal language, sign language, gestures, or assistive communication devices. Assessments might involve observing a student's communication attempts, evaluating their vocabulary and grammar skills, or assessing their ability to use communication devices.

- **Receptive Communication:** Receptive communication refers to a person's ability to understand the communication of others. This might involve understanding verbal language, sign language, gestures, or written words. Assessments might involve observing a student's responses to communication, evaluating their ability to follow directions, or assessing their comprehension of written materials.

Holistic, Person-Centered Assessment

Person-centered assessment puts the student at the center of the assessment process. It considers their individual strengths, needs, and preferences. This approach is essential for students with severe to profound disabilities.

- **Focus on Strengths:** Traditional assessments often focus on what a student can't do. Person-centered assessment focuses on what a student can do. By identifying a student's strengths, educators can build on those strengths to help them learn and grow.

- **Consider Individual Needs:** Each student has unique needs. Assessments should be tailored to meet those needs. This might involve modifying assessment procedures, providing accommodations, or using alternative assessment methods.

- **Respect Preferences:** Students should be involved in the assessment process as much as possible. Their preferences should be respected. This might involve allowing students to choose the activities they want to participate in or asking them for feedback on the assessment process.

Adaptive Assessment Tools and Methodologies

Adaptive assessment tools and methodologies adjust to the student's performance. This ensures that the assessment is challenging but not frustrating.

- **Dynamic Assessment:** Dynamic assessment is a type of adaptive assessment that involves providing support to the student during the assessment process. The educator observes how the student responds to the support and adjusts their approach accordingly. This helps identify the student's learning potential and the types of support they need to succeed.

- **Task Analysis:** Task analysis involves breaking down a complex task into smaller, more manageable steps. The educator then assesses the student's ability to complete each step. This helps identify specific areas where the student needs support and to provide targeted instruction.

- **Portfolio Assessment:** Portfolio assessment involves collecting samples of a student's work over time. This provides a holistic view of the student's abilities and progress. Portfolios can include a variety of materials, such as photographs, videos, artwork, and writing samples.

Examples of Adaptive Assessment Tools

Several adaptive assessment tools can be used with students with severe to profound disabilities.

- **The Assessment, Evaluation, and Programming System (AEPS):** The AEPS is a curriculum-based assessment system for children from birth to six years of age. It assesses development in several areas, including cognitive, motor, social-emotional, and adaptive skills. The AEPS is designed to be used in natural settings, such as the classroom or home.

- **The Vineland Adaptive Behavior Scales (VABS):** The VABS is a standardized assessment of adaptive behavior. It measures skills in four domains: communication, daily living skills, socialization, and motor skills. The VABS can be used with individuals from birth to adulthood.

- **The Communication Matrix:** The Communication Matrix is an assessment tool that helps identify the communication skills of individuals with severe communication impairments. It assesses a range of communication behaviors, from pre-intentional communication (such as crying or fussing) to symbolic communication (such as using words or signs).

By using these specialized assessment methods, educators can gain a better understanding of the strengths, needs, and preferences of students with severe to profound disabilities. This information can then be used to develop individualized education programs that promote their learning, development, and well-being. It's important to remember that assessment is an ongoing process, and that assessment methods should be adjusted as the student's needs change. The goal is to empower students to reach their full potential and participate meaningfully in their communities.

Strategic Data Collection Techniques

For educators working with students who have disabilities, especially those with severe to profound needs, gathering data in a systematic way and checking on progress is essential. It helps make sure teaching is effective and meets each student's specific needs. This involves using different ways to track information, from numbers and graphs to detailed notes and observations.

One important distinction is between quantitative and qualitative data. Quantitative data uses numbers to measure things, like how many times a student does something or how long it takes them to finish a task. Qualitative data, on the other hand, involves descriptive observations, like noting how a student interacts with others or how they approach a problem. Both types of data are helpful for getting a full picture of a student's learning and development.

When it comes to tracking data, there are a few common methods. Frequency counts involve recording how often a specific behavior happens within a certain time. This can be helpful for tracking things like how often a student initiates a conversation or how often they need help with a task. Duration recording measures how long a behavior lasts, which can be useful for tracking things like how long a student can stay focused on an activity. Interval recording involves dividing a period of time into smaller intervals and noting whether a behavior occurs during each interval. This can be helpful for tracking behaviors that happen frequently or inconsistently.

Another useful method is task analysis, which involves breaking down a complex task into smaller steps and recording whether a student can complete each step independently. This can help identify specific areas where a student needs support. For example, if a student is learning to brush their teeth, the task can be broken down into steps like getting the toothbrush, putting toothpaste on it, and brushing each section of the teeth.

In recent years, technology has provided new tools for tracking student progress. Electronic data collection systems can make it easier to record and analyze data, reducing the risk of errors and saving time. These systems often include features like automated graphing and reporting, which can help educators identify trends and make data-based decisions. Wearable devices can also be used to track things like a student's activity level or heart rate, providing additional information about their physical and emotional state.

Regardless of the method used, it's important to define behaviors clearly and consistently. This means using specific, observable language to describe what the behavior looks like. For example, instead of saying "the student is disruptive," it would be more helpful to say "the student gets out of their seat and walks around the classroom without permission." This makes it easier for different people to collect data in a consistent way.

To make sure the data is reliable, it's also a good idea to have two people collect data independently and then compare their results. This is known as inter-rater reliability. If the two people agree on the data most of the time, it increases confidence that the data is accurate.

Once data has been collected, it's important to create meaningful progress indicators. These are specific, measurable goals that reflect the student's individual needs and priorities. Progress indicators should be based on the student's current level of performance and should be challenging but achievable. For example, a progress indicator might be "the student will independently complete 3 out of 5 steps of a task analysis for washing their hands."

When setting goals, it's important to consider not only academic skills but also functional skills. Functional skills are those that a student needs to live independently and participate in their community. Examples include self-care skills, communication skills, and social skills.

Visual representations of data, like graphs and charts, can be helpful for tracking progress and communicating results to others. Graphs can show trends over time, making it easy to see whether a student is making progress toward their goals. Charts can be used to compare a student's performance to that of their peers or to track their progress across different areas.

Interpreting student performance data can be complex, especially when working with students who have multiple disabilities. It's important to consider all available information, including not only quantitative data but also qualitative observations and input from the student, their family, and other professionals.

When interpreting data, it's important to look for patterns and trends. Are there specific times of day or situations in which the student performs better or worse? Are there specific strategies or interventions that seem to be more effective than others? It's also important to consider any external factors that might be affecting the student's performance, such as changes in their medication or family situation.

Documenting incremental student achievements is also essential. This involves keeping a record of even small steps forward, which can help motivate the student and their team. Documentation can take many forms, including written notes, photographs, videos, and work samples.

One helpful strategy is to create a portfolio of the student's work. This can include examples of their best work, as well as examples that show their progress over time. The portfolio can be used to showcase the student's achievements and to communicate their progress to others.

Data collection plays a role in individualized educational planning. The data collected informs the development of the IEP. Regular data helps tailor teaching methods to meet specific needs, ensuring the IEP's goals are both relevant and attainable. Data helps track how well a student is doing, which is important for making decisions about their education plan. The IEP is reviewed regularly, and the data is essential in deciding if goals need adjusting or if new support should be added. This ensures the IEP stays effective and up-to-date.

For instance, consider a student with autism spectrum disorder who has difficulty with social interactions. Quantitative data might include the number of times the student initiates a conversation or responds to a greeting from a peer. Qualitative data might include observations of the student's body language and facial expressions during social interactions.

Based on this data, the IEP team might set a progress indicator such as "the student will initiate a conversation with a peer at least once per day, using appropriate eye contact and tone of voice." To track progress, the teacher might use a frequency count to record the number of times the student initiates a conversation. They might also take notes on the student's body language and facial expressions.

If the data shows that the student is not making progress toward their goal, the IEP team might decide to modify the intervention. This could involve providing more explicit instruction on social skills, using visual supports to help the student understand social cues, or creating opportunities for the student to practice social interactions in a structured setting.

By collecting and analyzing data in a systematic way, educators can make data-based decisions about instruction and intervention. This can help ensure that students with severe to profound disabilities are making progress toward their goals and reaching their full potential. Data collection supports collaboration among educators, therapists, and families, creating a unified approach to support the student's development. This collaboration is vital for consistent support across all environments.

In summary, effective data collection and progress monitoring are crucial for educators working with students with severe to profound disabilities. By using a variety of methods to track information, creating meaningful progress indicators, and interpreting data in a thoughtful way, educators can tailor instruction to meet individual needs and help students achieve their full potential. The use of technology, combined with consistent and reliable data collection practices, further enhances the ability to support these students effectively.

Navigating Assessment Legal Landscape

Legal and ethical considerations are cornerstones of special education assessment, protecting the rights of students while ensuring fair and accurate evaluations. These considerations guide every step of the assessment process, from initial referral to the interpretation of results, and shape how educators support students with disabilities.

Federal laws, particularly the Individuals with Disabilities Education Act (IDEA), lay the groundwork for special education assessment. IDEA mandates that students with disabilities receive a free appropriate public education (FAPE) in the least restrictive environment (LRE). This includes comprehensive evaluations to determine eligibility for special education services and to develop Individualized Education Programs (IEPs). IDEA emphasizes specific requirements for assessments, stipulating that they must be non-discriminatory, administered in the student's native language, and technically sound. The law also highlights the need for multiple assessment tools and strategies to gather relevant functional, developmental, and academic information about the student.

States often enact their own regulations that build upon federal law, providing additional detail and specificity. These state regulations may address timelines for assessment, qualifications for evaluators, and specific assessment instruments to be used. Staying abreast of both federal and state laws is vital for special education professionals. They can ensure they adhere to the latest requirements and guidelines. This adherence prevents legal challenges and promotes ethical practice.

Protecting student rights during the evaluation process is crucial. Informed consent is a central tenet, requiring that parents or guardians are fully informed about the assessment process and provide written permission before evaluations begin. This includes clear explanations of the purpose of the assessment, the types of tests or procedures to be used, and how the results will be used to inform educational planning. Parents have the right to review all assessment records and to obtain an independent educational evaluation (IEE) if they disagree with the school's evaluation. Schools must consider the results of IEEs, adding another layer of protection for student rights.

Confidentiality is another vital aspect of student rights. Assessment results and other personally identifiable information must be protected under the Family Educational Rights and Privacy Act (FERPA). This law restricts access to student records to authorized personnel and requires parental consent before disclosing information to third parties. Maintaining confidentiality builds trust between families and schools. It also helps to create a safe and supportive environment for students with disabilities.

Ensuring assessment fairness and non-discrimination is essential for equitable educational opportunities. Assessments must be free from cultural, linguistic, and other biases that could unfairly disadvantage students from diverse backgrounds. This requires selecting assessment tools that are appropriate for the student's age, language proficiency, and cultural background. Evaluators should be trained to recognize and address potential sources of bias in the assessment process.

Alternative assessment methods, such as portfolios, performance-based tasks, and observations, can provide a more complete picture of the student's abilities than standardized tests alone. These methods allow students to demonstrate their knowledge and skills in authentic contexts, reducing the reliance on traditional measures that may be biased or inappropriate. Also, accommodations and modifications should be provided to students during assessments to ensure that they have an equal opportunity to demonstrate their knowledge and skills. These might include extended time, breaks, or alternative formats.

Ethical guidelines for assessment professionals provide a framework for responsible and competent practice. Professional organizations, such as the Council for Exceptional Children (CEC) and the American Psychological Association (APA), have developed ethical codes that address assessment practices. These codes emphasize the importance of competence, integrity, responsibility, and respect for the rights and welfare of individuals.

Competence involves having the necessary knowledge, skills, and training to administer and interpret assessments accurately. Evaluators should only use assessment tools for which they have been properly trained and should stay up-to-date on current best practices in assessment. Integrity requires honesty, objectivity, and fairness in all aspects of the assessment process. Evaluators should avoid conflicts of interest and should not misrepresent assessment results.

Responsibility involves protecting the rights and welfare of students and families. Evaluators should obtain informed consent, maintain confidentiality, and use assessment results to benefit the student. They should also be aware of the limitations of assessment tools and should not make decisions based solely on test scores. Respect for the rights and welfare of individuals requires treating all students and families with dignity and respect. Evaluators should be sensitive to cultural and linguistic differences and should involve families in the assessment process.

The intersection of legal requirements and student-centered assessment practices is where effective special education thrives. Legal mandates provide the structure, while student-centered practices ensure the assessment process is tailored to the individual needs of each student. This involves using a variety of assessment methods, gathering data from multiple sources, and involving the student and their family in the assessment process.

Assessments should focus on identifying the student's strengths, interests, and learning preferences, as well as their needs. This information can then be used to develop an IEP that is tailored to the student's unique characteristics and goals. Student-centered assessment also involves ongoing monitoring of progress and adjustments to the IEP as needed.

The potential consequences of non-compliance with legal and ethical requirements can be severe. Schools may face legal challenges, such as due process hearings or lawsuits, if they violate student rights. These legal battles can be costly and time-consuming. They can also damage the school's reputation and erode trust with families.

Moreover, non-compliance can have negative impacts on students. Inaccurate or biased assessments can lead to inappropriate educational placements and services, which can hinder student progress and limit their opportunities. Students may also experience emotional distress if they are subjected to unfair or discriminatory assessment practices.

Best practices for maintaining ethical standards in special education assessment include ongoing training and professional development for evaluators, clear and transparent communication with families, and a commitment to using assessment results to benefit students. Schools should establish policies and procedures that ensure compliance with legal and ethical requirements. They should also create a culture of respect for student rights and diversity.

Regular audits of assessment practices can help to identify and address potential problems. These audits should involve a review of assessment records, interviews with evaluators and teachers, and feedback from families. By taking a proactive approach to ethical compliance, schools can protect student rights. They can also promote fair and effective assessment practices.

Consider a scenario where a student with a learning disability is referred for special education assessment. The school psychologist, following ethical guidelines, obtains informed consent from the parents before beginning the evaluation. The psychologist uses a variety of assessment tools, including standardized tests, classroom observations, and work samples, to gather information about the student's academic skills and learning style.

The psychologist also considers the student's cultural and linguistic background when interpreting the assessment results. They recognize that the student's limited English proficiency may affect their performance on standardized tests. The psychologist collaborates with the student's teachers and parents to develop an IEP that addresses the student's specific needs and strengths.

In another scenario, a student with autism spectrum disorder exhibits challenging behaviors in the classroom. The special education team conducts a Functional Behavior Assessment (FBA) to identify the triggers and functions of the behaviors. The FBA includes observations, interviews, and data collection to understand the context in which the behaviors occur.

Based on the FBA results, the team develops a Behavior Intervention Plan (BIP) that includes positive behavior supports and strategies to teach the student alternative behaviors. The BIP is implemented consistently across all settings, and data is collected to monitor the student's progress. The team regularly reviews and modifies the BIP as needed to ensure its effectiveness.

These scenarios show the practical application of legal and ethical considerations in special education assessment. By following these guidelines, educators can ensure that all students have the opportunity to receive a fair and appropriate education.

Technology also influences how data is handled and secured. Implementing strong cybersecurity measures to protect student data is essential, especially with the increasing use of electronic data collection systems. Training staff on data privacy and security protocols is equally important.

Regularly updating assessment tools and practices to reflect advances in technology and changes in legal standards ensures that assessments remain effective and fair. Embracing technology, while prioritizing ethical data handling, enhances the assessment process.

In summary, legal and ethical considerations are vital to special education assessment. IDEA and state regulations set the framework, while ethical guidelines provide a moral compass for professionals. By protecting student rights, ensuring fairness, and maintaining ethical standards, educators can create equitable and supportive learning environments for all students with disabilities. A proactive and informed approach to legal and ethical compliance not only avoids legal challenges but also fosters trust and enhances educational outcomes for students.

4

ETHICS PROFESSIONALISM AND COLLABORATION

Special Education Legal Landscape

The field of special education is guided by a complex web of laws designed to protect the rights of students with disabilities and ensure they receive a free and appropriate public education. These laws provide a framework for identifying, assessing, and educating students with disabilities, including those with severe to profound disabilities. Understanding this legal landscape is essential for educators, administrators, and parents alike, as it dictates the responsibilities of schools and the rights of students.

One must understand how special education laws evolved to fully grasp their present-day significance. The Individuals with Disabilities Education Act (IDEA), originally enacted as the Education for All Handicapped Children Act in 1975, stands as the cornerstone of special education law in the United States. Before this landmark legislation, many children with disabilities were excluded from public schools or received inadequate educational services. IDEA mandates that all states provide a free and appropriate public education (FAPE) to eligible children with disabilities, regardless of the severity of their disability. The law has been amended several times since its original enactment, with each reauthorization strengthening and refining the rights and protections afforded to students with disabilities. These reauthorizations clarified eligibility criteria, emphasized the importance of individualized education programs (IEPs), and promoted the inclusion of students with disabilities in the general education setting to the greatest extent appropriate.

IDEA comprises four key parts, each addressing distinct aspects of special education. Part A outlines the general provisions of the law, defining key terms and establishing the national policy for educating students with disabilities. Part B details the requirements for states and local educational agencies (LEAs) to provide FAPE to eligible children with disabilities aged 3 through 21. This includes provisions for identification, evaluation, IEP development, placement in the least restrictive environment (LRE), and procedural safeguards for parents. Part C focuses on early intervention services for infants and toddlers with disabilities and their families. This section emphasizes family-centered services and supports to promote the child's development and prepare them for school. Finally, Part D addresses national activities to support the improvement of special education, including research, technical assistance, and personnel development.

Beyond IDEA, other federal laws play a vital role in protecting the rights of students with disabilities. The Americans with Disabilities Act (ADA) prohibits discrimination based on disability in various settings, including schools, workplaces, and public accommodations. Title II of the ADA specifically applies to public entities, including public schools, ensuring that students with disabilities have equal access to educational programs and activities. Section 504 of the Rehabilitation Act of 1973 is another essential piece of legislation. It prohibits discrimination based on disability in programs and activities receiving federal funding, which includes nearly all public schools. Section 504 requires schools to provide reasonable accommodations to students with disabilities to ensure they can participate fully in the educational program. These accommodations may include modifications to the curriculum, assistive technology, or other supports.

It's also important to examine the specific legal protections afforded to students with severe disabilities under these laws. IDEA, ADA, and Section 504 collectively ensure that students with severe disabilities have the right to FAPE, access to the general education curriculum to the maximum extent appropriate, and reasonable accommodations to support their learning. FAPE, as defined by IDEA, means special education and related services that are provided at public expense, under public supervision and direction, and without charge; meet the standards of the state educational agency; include an appropriate preschool, elementary school, or secondary school education in the state involved; and are provided in conformity with an IEP. The IEP is a legally binding document that outlines the student's educational goals, the special education and related services they will receive, and the accommodations and modifications necessary to support their learning. For students with severe disabilities, the IEP must address their unique needs, including communication, mobility, self-care, and social skills.

The legal obligations of educational institutions extend beyond simply providing access to education; they also encompass mandatory procedural and substantive legal requirements. Procedural safeguards under IDEA ensure that parents have the right to participate in all aspects of their child's special education. This includes the right to receive notice of proposed actions, to consent to evaluations and services, to participate in IEP meetings, and to challenge school decisions through mediation or due process hearings. Substantive requirements under IDEA mandate that schools provide FAPE in the LRE. This means that students with disabilities should be educated with their non-disabled peers to the greatest extent appropriate, and removal from the general education setting should occur only when the nature or severity of the disability is such that education in regular classes with the use of supplementary aids and services cannot be achieved satisfactorily.

Consider the following scenarios to illustrate these legal concepts:

- **Case Study 1: Access to Communication** - A student with cerebral palsy and limited verbal communication is denied access to an augmentative and alternative communication (AAC) device by the school district, arguing it's too expensive. The parents file a complaint, citing IDEA's mandate for related services and assistive technology. The hearing officer rules in favor of the parents, stating the AAC device is necessary for the student to access FAPE.

- **Case Study 2: Inclusive Education** - A high school student with Down syndrome is placed in a segregated special education classroom for all subjects. The parents advocate for increased inclusion in general education classes, with appropriate supports and modifications. The IEP team agrees to gradually increase the student's participation in general education classes, providing necessary supports such as co-teaching and peer tutoring.

- **Case Study 3: Behavioral Supports** - A student with autism spectrum disorder exhibits challenging behaviors in the classroom, leading to frequent suspensions. The school implements a Positive Behavior Support (PBS) plan based on a Functional Behavior Assessment (FBA). The PBS plan includes strategies for preventing challenging behaviors, teaching replacement behaviors, and providing positive reinforcement. The student's behavior improves, and suspensions are no longer necessary.

These cases demonstrate the practical implications of special education laws for students with severe disabilities, educators, and administrators. They highlight the importance of individualized assessment, appropriate supports and services, and the right to meaningful participation in the educational process.

Connecting these legal frameworks to the broader themes of inclusive, student-centered special education underscores their significance. The legal mandates of IDEA, ADA, and Section 504 support the principles of inclusion, individualized instruction, and student empowerment. These laws provide a foundation for creating educational environments that are accessible, supportive, and responsive to the unique needs of all learners. By understanding and adhering to these legal requirements, educators can ensure that students with severe disabilities have the opportunity to reach their full potential and participate meaningfully in their communities. The laws are not just regulations but instruments to enable just, equitable, and quality education for all students, thereby knitting together the varied threads of special education into a robust, legally sound, and ethically driven framework.

Ethical Decision-Making in Special Education

Working with students who have severe to profound disabilities brings unique ethical questions that demand careful thought. These questions often involve balancing the student's rights, their needs, legal rules, and what educators believe is right.

Special education teachers must know the ethical guidelines that guide their work. Organizations like the Council for Exceptional Children (CEC) have created codes of ethics that offer direction on how to act responsibly and fairly. These standards cover a wide range of topics, like keeping student information private, getting permission for actions, and treating all students with respect and dignity. They also stress the importance of working together with families and other professionals to create the best possible results for students. These ethical standards serve as a roadmap, helping educators make decisions that support the well-being and rights of their students.

Educators in special education often face situations that test their moral principles. Imagine a student needs a specific type of therapy to help them communicate, but the school says it doesn't have the money to provide it. What should the teacher do? Or, think about a student whose parents disagree on the best way to handle their child's behavior problems. How can the teacher balance the parents' wishes while still doing what's best for the student? These kinds of dilemmas don't have easy answers. They call for a careful look at all sides of the issue, along with a strong dedication to doing what is morally right. Teachers have to weigh different values, like the student's right to get the services they need, the school's responsibility to manage its resources, and the parents' role in making decisions about their child's education.

Another tricky ethical area is keeping student information private and getting proper permission for actions. Students with severe to profound disabilities might not be able to give informed consent themselves, making it even more important for educators to protect their privacy and involve their families in decisions. This means only sharing student information with people who need to know it, like other teachers or therapists, and always getting permission from parents or guardians before doing things like taking photos or videos of the student. It also means explaining things in a way that the student and their family can understand, so they can make informed choices about their education and care. Educators must stay updated on privacy laws like the Family Educational Rights and Privacy Act (FERPA), which give specific instructions on how to handle student records and protect their privacy rights.

Teachers' own values and beliefs can also play a role in ethical decision-making. Everyone has their own sense of what's right and wrong, and this can influence how they approach ethical dilemmas. It's important for educators to be aware of their own biases and to make sure they're not letting their personal beliefs get in the way of doing what's best for the student. For example, a teacher might have strong feelings about a certain type of therapy, but they need to be open to other approaches if those are more appropriate for the student. Setting clear professional boundaries is also key. Teachers should avoid getting too personally involved with students or their families, as this could cloud their judgment and make it harder to make objective decisions. By maintaining a professional distance, teachers can make sure they're always acting in the student's best interest.

To deal with these kinds of ethical challenges, educators need a structured way of thinking through the issues and coming to a decision. Here's one possible approach:

1. **Identify the ethical problem.** What are the different values or principles that are clashing in this situation? Who is affected by the decision?

2. **Gather information.** Get all the facts you can about the situation. Talk to the student, their family, and other professionals involved. Look at any relevant laws, policies, or ethical guidelines.

3. **Consider different options.** What are all the possible courses of action you could take? What are the pros and cons of each option?

4. **Apply ethical principles.** Think about which ethical principles are most relevant to this situation. Are you prioritizing the student's autonomy, their well-being, or their right to privacy?

5. **Make a decision.** Based on all the information you've gathered, choose the course of action that you believe is most ethical. Be prepared to explain your reasoning.

6. **Evaluate the results.** After you've taken action, take some time to reflect on what happened. Did you achieve the outcome you were hoping for? What did you learn from this experience?

Here are some specific examples of how this decision-making framework could be applied in real-world scenarios:

- **Scenario:** A student with a severe intellectual disability is engaging in self-injurious behavior, such as hitting their head against a wall. The parents are hesitant to use restrictive interventions, such as physical restraints, but the teacher is concerned about the student's safety.

- **Ethical problem:** Balancing the student's right to autonomy with the teacher's responsibility to protect them from harm.

- **Information gathering:** The teacher consults with the parents, a behavior specialist, and the school psychologist. They review the student's IEP and any relevant policies on the use of restrictive interventions.

- **Options:** The teacher could try using positive reinforcement strategies to reduce the self-injurious behavior, implement environmental modifications to make the environment safer, or use physical restraints as a last resort.

- **Ethical principles:** The teacher considers the principles of beneficence (doing good), non-maleficence (avoiding harm), and respect for autonomy.

- **Decision:** The teacher decides to implement a positive behavior support plan that focuses on teaching the student alternative ways to communicate their needs. They also make changes to the classroom environment to reduce triggers for the self-injurious behavior. Physical restraints are only used as a last resort, when the student is in immediate danger of harming themselves.

- **Evaluation:** The teacher regularly monitors the student's behavior and adjusts the intervention plan as needed. They also communicate regularly with the parents to keep them informed of the student's progress.

- **Scenario:** A student with a profound disability is nonverbal and relies on assistive technology to communicate. The teacher suspects that the student is being abused at home, but the student is unable to communicate directly about the abuse.

- **Ethical problem:** Balancing the teacher's duty to report suspected child abuse with the student's right to privacy and confidentiality.

- **Information gathering:** The teacher observes the student closely for any signs of abuse, such as unexplained injuries or changes in behavior. They also consult with the school counselor and the principal.

- **Options:** The teacher could report their suspicions to child protective services, or they could wait and gather more evidence before taking action.

- **Ethical principles:** The teacher considers the principles of beneficence (protecting the student from harm) and justice (ensuring that the student's rights are protected).

- **Decision:** The teacher decides to report their suspicions to child protective services, as they believe that the student's safety is at risk.

- **Evaluation:** The teacher cooperates fully with the child protective services investigation. They also provide support to the student and their family, as needed.

Ethical decision-making is not always easy, but it is an essential part of being a special education teacher. By understanding ethical frameworks, considering different perspectives, and using a structured approach to problem-solving, educators can make choices that support the well-being and rights of their students with severe to profound disabilities.

Collaborative Educational Partnerships

Building successful teamwork is very important in special education, especially when helping students with significant disabilities.

Stakeholder Mapping

To start, it's vital to know who the key players are. These individuals, or stakeholders, are the people who have a direct interest or influence in the student's education and well-being. These usually include the student's family, educators, therapists, healthcare providers, and any community support services involved.

- **Families:** Families are usually the most important members of the team. They hold crucial information about the student's history, preferences, strengths, and needs. They are also legally responsible for making important decisions about the student's education and care.

- **Educators:** This group is composed of special education teachers, general education teachers, paraprofessionals, and any other school staff who work directly with the student. They are responsible for creating and implementing the student's Individualized Education Program (IEP), adapting the curriculum to meet the student's needs, and providing a supportive learning environment.

- **Therapists:** Occupational therapists, physical therapists, speech-language pathologists, and behavioral therapists bring specialized skills to help students reach particular goals. Occupational therapists help with everyday living and fine motor skills. Physical therapists work on movement and balance. Speech-language pathologists address communication and swallowing difficulties, while behavioral therapists work to address behavioral issues.

- **Healthcare Providers:** Doctors, nurses, and other medical experts provide essential healthcare services. They help manage the student's medical issues, provide medical information to the team, and work together to coordinate care.

- **Community Support Services:** Different community organizations can offer extra help to students and their families. These may include social workers, support groups, vocational rehabilitation services, and recreational programs.

Once you identify the stakeholders, consider mapping their involvement and influence. This means understanding each member's role, responsibilities, and how they interact with one another. For example, how often does the family communicate with the teacher? How well do the therapists and educators work together to achieve common goals? Map the current situation to find possible gaps or areas for improvement.

Scenario: A student named Sarah has cerebral palsy and uses a wheelchair. Her team includes her parents, her special education teacher, a physical therapist, and an occupational therapist. By mapping out the team's roles, it becomes clear that communication between the therapists and the parents is limited. To address this, the team decides to schedule regular meetings where the therapists can update the parents on Sarah's progress and get their input on goals and strategies.

Communication Strategies

Good communication is the glue that holds a team together. It involves sharing information clearly, listening actively, and respecting diverse perspectives. Here are a few tips for improving communication within special education teams:

- **Active Listening:** When someone is talking, focus on understanding their point of view before sharing your own. Pay attention to both verbal and nonverbal cues, and ask clarifying questions.

- **Empathetic Communication:** Put yourself in the other person's shoes and try to understand their emotions and experiences. Use language that shows empathy and compassion. For example, instead of saying, "I don't think that's a good idea," try saying, "I understand your perspective, and I'm wondering if we could consider some other options as well."

- **Clear and Concise Language:** Avoid jargon and technical terms that others may not understand. Use clear, simple language to express your ideas. Provide specific examples and avoid generalizations.

- **Regular Meetings:** Schedule regular team meetings to discuss the student's progress, address any challenges, and plan for the future. These meetings should be structured and focused, with clear agendas and action items.

- **Technology Tools:** Use technology to improve communication and collaboration. Email, video conferencing, and online collaboration platforms can help team members stay connected and share information easily.

- **Conflict Resolution:** Disagreements are inevitable in any team. When conflicts arise, address them directly and respectfully. Focus on finding solutions that meet the needs of everyone involved.

- **Written Communication:** Use emails and reports to document important information, decisions, and action items. This helps ensure that everyone is on the same page and can refer back to previous discussions.

Scenario: During an IEP meeting for a student with autism, the parents express frustration with the student's lack of progress in social skills. The teacher listens attentively, acknowledges their concerns, and asks clarifying questions to understand their perspective. Together, they brainstorm new strategies and set measurable goals for improving the student's social interactions.

Collaborative Planning

When team members work together to create support plans, it ensures that everyone is working towards the same goals and that the student gets the help they require. This involves integrating different areas of knowledge, sharing resources, and coordinating activities.

- **Shared Goal Setting:** Work together to create shared goals that are important to the student, their family, and the educational team. These goals should be based on the student's strengths, needs, and interests, and should be measurable and achievable.

- **Integrated Support Plans:** Create support plans that incorporate the knowledge and skills of all team members. For example, a physical therapist might work with the teacher to adapt classroom activities to meet the student's physical needs. A speech-language pathologist might work with the family to implement communication strategies at home.

- **Coordinated Activities:** Coordinate activities and interventions to avoid duplication of effort and ensure that the student receives consistent support. For example, if the student is working on a particular skill in therapy, the teacher can reinforce that skill in the classroom.

- **Resource Sharing:** Share resources and materials to support the student's learning and development. This might include adaptive equipment, assistive technology, or specialized instructional materials.

- **Regular Evaluation:** Regularly evaluate the effectiveness of the support plan and make adjustments as needed. This involves collecting data on the student's progress, soliciting feedback from team members, and making changes to the plan based on the results.

- **Family-Centered Approach**: Make sure the family is at the center of the planning process. Respect their values, priorities, and cultural background. Involve them in all decisions about the student's education and care.

Scenario: A student with Down syndrome is struggling to learn to read. The team, including the special education teacher, a reading specialist, and the parents, collaborates to design an integrated support plan. The reading specialist provides evidence-based reading interventions, the teacher reinforces these interventions in the classroom, and the parents read with the student at home every night. Together, they monitor the student's progress and make changes to the plan as needed.

Cultural Competence

In special education, cultural competence means respecting diversity and understanding that each family is different. This means recognizing that cultural background, language, values, and beliefs can all affect how families interact with the educational system. To be successful, you need to learn about different cultures, understand your own biases, and change your methods to meet the needs of diverse families.

- **Cultural Awareness:** Take the time to learn about different cultures and how they might affect a family's values, beliefs, and practices. This might involve reading books, attending workshops, or talking to people from different cultures.

* **Self-Reflection:** Think about your own cultural biases and assumptions. How might these biases affect how you interact with families from different cultures? Be willing to challenge your own beliefs and assumptions.

* **Open Communication:** Communicate openly and respectfully with families from different cultures. Ask questions to understand their perspectives and avoid making assumptions. Be willing to listen and learn.

* **Flexibility:** Be willing to change your methods to meet the needs of families from different cultures. This might involve adapting your communication style, modifying your instructional materials, or providing support in the family's native language.

* **Collaboration:** Work with cultural liaisons or community organizations to bridge cultural gaps and provide culturally sensitive support to families.

* **Respect:** Show respect for the family's values, beliefs, and practices. Avoid making judgments or imposing your own values on them.

Scenario: A student from a refugee family has recently enrolled in a special education program. The teacher recognizes that the family may have experienced trauma and may have different cultural values and beliefs. The teacher works with a cultural liaison to learn more about the family's background and to develop a culturally sensitive support plan.

Effective teamwork is not just about following the rules or doing what is expected. It is about building real relationships, appreciating differences, and working together to help students with significant disabilities reach their full capacity. By mapping stakeholders, improving communication, planning collaboratively, and being culturally sensitive, special education teams can make a positive impact on the lives of students and their families.

Professional Growth and Advocacy

Ongoing professional development is not just recommended but essential for special education teachers, particularly those working with students who have severe to profound disabilities. To provide the most effective support, educators must keep up with the latest evidence-based practices, emerging technologies, and evolving legal and ethical standards.

One way to stay current is by actively engaging with the research. Instead of simply reading summaries or attending occasional workshops, teachers can develop a system for regularly reviewing new research in their field. This might involve subscribing to journals, setting up Google Scholar alerts for specific keywords, or participating in online professional learning communities. When reading research, it's important to critically evaluate the study's methodology, sample size, and findings before applying them to classroom practice.

Another strategy is to seek out professional development opportunities that focus on specific areas of need. These can range from short workshops to multi-day conferences. When choosing professional development, teachers should look for programs that are evidence-based, interactive, and relevant to their students' needs. It's also helpful to attend programs that offer opportunities for networking and collaboration with other educators.

Certification is a formal way to show expertise and commitment to the field. The Council for Exceptional Children (CEC) offers several certifications for special education teachers, including the general curriculum and adapted curriculum certifications. These certifications require teachers to demonstrate knowledge and skills in areas such as assessment, instruction, and classroom management. They can lead to career advancement and increased earning potential.

Advanced training, like earning a master's or doctoral degree, provides opportunities for in-depth study and specialization. Graduate programs in special education typically offer concentrations in areas such as autism, intellectual disabilities, or early intervention. These programs prepare teachers for leadership roles in schools and districts. They help teachers develop research skills, advanced knowledge of instructional strategies, and the ability to advocate for students with disabilities.

Specialization is a more focused way to develop expertise in a particular area. For example, a teacher might specialize in assistive technology, positive behavior supports, or transition services. Specialization can involve completing coursework, attending workshops, or earning a certificate in a specific area. It enables teachers to provide more targeted and effective support to students with specific needs.

Beyond individual development, educators can become advocates for systemic change. Systemic advocacy involves working to change policies, practices, and systems that affect students with disabilities. This can take many forms, from speaking out at school board meetings to lobbying legislators to participating in research.

Teachers can promote policy changes by becoming involved in professional organizations such as the CEC or the Autism Society. These organizations advocate for policies that support students with disabilities and their families. Teachers can also advocate for policy changes at the local level by working with school administrators, school boards, and community leaders.

Educational equity can be pursued by making sure that all students have access to high-quality education, regardless of their disability, race, ethnicity, or socioeconomic status. Teachers can promote educational equity by using culturally responsive teaching practices, differentiating instruction to meet the needs of all learners, and advocating for equitable funding and resources for special education programs.

Self-care and resilience are often overlooked in the field of special education, yet they are essential for teachers' well-being and effectiveness. The demands of the job can lead to burnout, stress, and emotional exhaustion. Without strategies for managing these challenges, teachers may experience decreased job satisfaction, impaired performance, and even physical and mental health problems.

One strategy for addressing professional burnout is to practice self-care regularly. This might involve setting aside time for activities that promote relaxation, such as exercise, meditation, or spending time in nature. It might also involve engaging in hobbies, spending time with loved ones, or seeking therapy or counseling.

Another strategy is to build resilience, which is the ability to bounce back from adversity. Resilience can be developed by cultivating positive relationships, practicing gratitude, and developing a sense of purpose. Teachers can also build resilience by setting realistic goals, managing their time effectively, and seeking support from colleagues and mentors.

Maintaining emotional well-being is crucial for special education teachers. This involves developing healthy coping mechanisms for dealing with stress, practicing self-compassion, and setting boundaries between work and personal life. Teachers can also promote emotional well-being by seeking supervision or consultation from experienced professionals, participating in peer support groups, or engaging in mindfulness practices.

This book has covered essential topics, from understanding developmental theories and learning differences to planning instruction, conducting assessments, and navigating the legal and ethical landscape. Now, as we reach the end, it's time to put this knowledge into action and see your role as more than just a job. It's a chance to really change things for students and their families.

As teachers, we are in a unique position to help students with severe to profound disabilities. We see them every day, learn about their strengths and needs, and build relationships with them. We can use this knowledge to create learning experiences that are not only effective but also meaningful and engaging. We can show the students that they are valued, respected, and capable of achieving their goals.

It's important to remember that special education is not just about academics. It's about helping students develop the skills they need to live fulfilling and independent lives. This might involve teaching them how to communicate, how to take care of themselves, how to interact with others, or how to find employment. As teachers, we must be creative and resourceful in finding ways to teach these skills and support students as they transition into adulthood.

But our job doesn't end in the classroom. We also have a responsibility to advocate for students with disabilities and their families. This might involve educating others about the needs of students with disabilities, working to change policies that discriminate against students with disabilities, or supporting organizations that advocate for students with disabilities. By being strong voices for the students, we can create a more inclusive and equitable society for all.

Change starts with each of us. We can decide to approach each day with a renewed sense of purpose and dedication. We can commit to learning new things, trying new strategies, and never giving up on our students. We can support each other, share our experiences, and celebrate our successes. By working together, we can make a huge difference in the lives of students with disabilities and create a future where all students have the opportunity to reach their full capacity.

5.1 FULL-LENGTH PRACTICE TEST 1

Section 1: Human Development and Individualized Learning Differences

Theories of Human Development

1. Which of the following best describes Lev Vygotsky's theory of cognitive development and its application in special education?

A) Children pass through four fixed stages of cognitive development based on age.

B) Learning is a social process, and children develop through interactions with more knowledgeable others.

C) Intelligence is fixed, and children with disabilities have limited learning potential.

D) Students should only be taught within their independent functioning level.

Understanding Intellectual and Developmental Disabilities (IDD)

2. Which of the following is a primary characteristic of students with severe to profound intellectual disabilities?

A) They typically demonstrate strong abstract reasoning skills.

B) They exhibit age-appropriate adaptive behaviors.

C) They often require significant support in daily living skills.

D) They learn at the same pace as their typically developing peers.

Impact of Disabilities on Learning

3. Which factor most significantly affects the academic learning of students with severe to profound disabilities?

A) Their motivation to complete assignments

B) Their access to assistive technology

C) The presence of co-occurring medical conditions

D) The strict adherence to traditional instructional strategies

Individualized Learning Needs

4. Which instructional approach is most effective for addressing the individualized learning needs of students with severe disabilities?

A) Whole-class direct instruction without modifications

B) Task analysis and systematic instruction tailored to each student

C) Standardized tests to measure learning progress

D) Independent self-study with limited teacher support

Section 2: Planning and Instruction and the Learning Environment

Developing Individualized Education Programs (IEPs)

5. What is the primary purpose of an Individualized Education Program (IEP)?

A) To provide a general education curriculum for all students

B) To set individualized goals and outline services for students with disabilities

C) To diagnose learning disabilities in students

D) To assess school performance based on standardized test scores

Instructional Strategies for Severe to Profound Disabilities

6. Which instructional approach is most effective for teaching communication skills to students with severe to profound disabilities?

A) Repetitive worksheets focusing on phonics

B) The use of Augmentative and Alternative Communication (AAC) devices

C) Group lectures without individualized modifications

D) Delayed reinforcement to encourage speech development

Classroom and Environmental Modifications

7. A teacher is designing a classroom for students with severe disabilities. Which of the following modifications would best support student learning and engagement?

A) Removing all visual supports to encourage independent learning

B) Providing a structured, predictable environment with clear visual schedules

C) Minimizing movement by limiting seating options to traditional desks

D) Using only verbal instructions without additional supports

Behavioral Interventions and Classroom Management

8. A student with profound disabilities exhibits frequent self-injurious behaviors. What is the most appropriate first step in addressing this behavior?

A) Implementing a punishment-based approach to stop the behavior

B) Conducting a Functional Behavior Assessment (FBA) to identify triggers

C) Ignoring the behavior to prevent reinforcement

D) Removing the student from the classroom permanently

Section 3: Assessment

Types of Assessments in Special Education

9. Which type of assessment is most appropriate for evaluating the functional skills of students with severe to profound disabilities?

A) Standardized norm-referenced tests

B) Functional and curriculum-based assessments

C) Multiple-choice exams with strict time limits

D) Verbal assessments without modifications

Assessing Students with Severe to Profound Disabilities

10. A teacher needs to assess a nonverbal student with severe disabilities. Which assessment approach is most appropriate?

A) Written tests requiring long responses

B) Direct observation and performance-based assessments

C) Multiple-choice exams with limited visual aids

D) Computer-based assessments with no accommodations

Data Collection and Progress Monitoring

11. Which data collection method is most effective for tracking progress in students with severe disabilities?

A) Occasional teacher observations without documentation

B) Systematic data collection using checklists, graphs, and anecdotal records

C) Only relying on annual IEP reviews

D) Using one-time assessments at the end of the school year

Legal and Ethical Considerations in Assessment

12. Under the Individuals with Disabilities Education Act (IDEA), how must assessments for students with disabilities be conducted?

A) In a language and format the student understands

B) Only using standardized English-based tests

C) In a setting with no accommodations or modifications

D) Without input from parents or special education professionals

Section 4: Ethical and Legal Practice, Professionalism, and Collaboration

Special Education Laws and Regulations

13. Which law ensures that students with disabilities receive a Free Appropriate Public Education (FAPE) in the Least Restrictive Environment (LRE)?

A) Section 504 of the Rehabilitation Act

B) Americans with Disabilities Act (AD A)

C) Individuals with Disabilities Education Act (IDEA)

D) Family Educational Rights and Privacy Act (FERP A)

Ethical Responsibilities in Special Education

14. A special education teacher is concerned about a colleague failing to implement IEP accommodations for a student. What is the most ethical course of action?

A) Ignore the situation to maintain a good working relationship

B) Immediately report the colleague to the principal without discussion

C) Discuss concerns with the colleague and collaborate to ensure compliance

D) Withdraw from the student's case to avoid involvement

Collaboration with Stakeholders

15. Which strategy is most effective for fostering collaboration between special education teachers and general education teachers?

A) Keeping IEP information confidential from general education teachers

B) Holding regular co-planning meetings to align instructional strategies

C) Allowing general education teachers to modify IEPs independently

D) Expecting general education teachers to manage all accommodations without support

Advocacy and Professional Development

16. A teacher wants to stay updated on best practices in special education. Which of the following would be the most beneficial professional development activity?

A) Attending special education conferences and workshops

B) Relying solely on personal classroom experience

C) Avoiding professional training due to a busy schedule

D) Using outdated materials without continuing education

Section 1: Human Development and Individualized Learning Differences

Theories of Human Development

17. According to Jean Piaget's theory of cognitive development, which stage is characterized by a child's ability to think logically about concrete events but struggles with abstract thinking?

A) Sensorimotor Stage

B) Preoperational Stage

C) Concrete Operational Stage

D) Formal Operational Stage

Understanding Intellectual and Developmental Disabilities (IDD)

18. Which of the following is a common characteristic of students with severe intellectual disabilities?

A) Strong independent problem-solving skills

B) Limited ability to generalize learned skills to new settings

C) High level of academic achievement with minimal support

D) Ability to perform tasks at the same level as peers with mild disabilities

Impact of Disabilities on Learning

19. A student with a severe intellectual disability is having difficulty maintaining attention during classroom instruction. Which of the following strategies is most effective in supporting the student's engagement?

A) Providing long lectures without visual support

B) Using short, structured activities with frequent breaks

C) Eliminating breaks to encourage focus

D) Providing only written instructions without modifications

Individualized Learning Needs

20. Which of the following instructional methods best supports individualized learning for students with severe to profound disabilities?

A) A one-size-fits-all curriculum

B) Personalized learning plans based on student strengths and needs

C) Sole reliance on verbal instruction

D) Passive learning with minimal interaction

Section 2: Planning and Instruction and the Learning Environment

Developing Individualized Education Programs (IEPs)

21. Which component is essential in writing an effective IEP goal?

A) Broad and vague language to allow flexibility

B) Specific, measurable, achievable, relevant, and time-bound (SMART) criteria

C) Goals that remain unchanged throughout the student's education

D) A focus only on academic subjects without considering life skills

Instructional Strategies for Severe to Profound Disabilities

22. A teacher is implementing a task analysis approach for teaching a student how to wash hands. What is the first step in using task analysis effectively?

A) Provide verbal instructions without modeling

B) Break down the skill into small, sequential steps

C) Expect the student to complete the task independently from the beginning

D) Allow the student to observe others without engaging in the task

Classroom and Environmental Modifications

23. What is the primary benefit of using visual schedules in classrooms for students with severe disabilities?

A) They increase reliance on verbal prompts

B) They help students understand and anticipate daily routines

C) They reduce the need for individualized instruction

D) They replace the need for teacher support

Behavioral Interventions and Classroom Management

24. A student with severe disabilities engages in self-stimulatory behaviors that interfere with learning. What is the best approach to addressing this behavior?

A) Ignoring the behavior completely

B) Providing alternative, functionally equivalent replacement behaviors

C) Using punishment-based strategies

D) Removing the student from the classroom permanently

Section 3: Assessment

Types of Assessments in Special Education

25. Which type of assessment is most appropriate for measuring a student's progress toward achieving their IEP goals?

A) Standardized norm-referenced tests

B) Curriculum-based assessments (CBAs)

C) High-stakes state testing

D) Teacher observations without documentation

Assessing Students with Severe to Profound Disabilities

26. Which assessment method is most appropriate for evaluating communication skills in a nonverbal student with severe disabilities?

A) Asking the student to verbally respond to questions

B) Using adaptive communication tools and structured observations

C) Relying solely on standardized test scores

D) Only interviewing parents about the student's skills

Data Collection and Progress Monitoring

27. A teacher is tracking a student's progress toward mastering self-care skills. Which data collection method would be most effective?

A) Conducting an annual assessment

B) Using a frequency recording chart to document progress daily

C) Relying only on parent reports

D) Using a single assessment at the end of the term

Legal and Ethical Considerations in Assessment

28. According to IDEA, assessments for students with disabilities must be conducted:

A) Using only standardized tests

B) In the student's primary language or communication mode

C) Without accommodations to ensure fairness

D) Only by general education teachers

Section 4: Ethical and Legal Practice, Professionalism, and Collaboration

Special Education Laws and Regulations

29. Which of the following is a primary goal of the Least Restrictive Environment (LRE) provision in IDEA?

A) To place all students with disabilities in general education classrooms without support

B) To ensure that students with disabilities are educated alongside peers to the greatest extent possible

C) To separate students with severe disabilities into specialized schools

D) To remove the need for accommodations in mainstream settings

Ethical Responsibilities in Special Education

30. A special education teacher is reviewing a student's IEP with the student's family. Which of the following represents the teacher's ethical responsibility?

A) Making major changes to the IEP without consulting the IEP team

B) Ensuring that the family fully understands the IEP and their rights

C) Keeping all educational decisions strictly in the hands of administrators

D) Ignoring parental concerns to avoid conflict

Collaboration with Stakeholders

31. What is the best approach for a special education teacher to build positive relationships with general education teachers?

A) Requiring general education teachers to manage special education needs independently

B) Regularly co-planning lessons and sharing resources

C) Avoiding communication to reduce workload

D) Limiting support to special education students only

Advocacy and Professional Development

32. A teacher wants to stay informed about new research in special education. What is the most effective way to do so?

A) Attending professional development workshops and conferences

B) Avoiding research due to time constraints

C) Relying only on personal teaching experience

D) Using outdated instructional methods

Section 1: Human Development and Individualized Learning Differences

Theories of Human Development

33. According to Erik Erikson's psychosocial development theory, what is the key developmental challenge faced by adolescents?

A) Developing trust vs. mistrust

B) Establishing initiative vs. guilt

C) Forming identity vs. role confusion

D) Achieving intimacy vs. isolation

Understanding Intellectual and Developmental Disabilities (IDD)

34. Which of the following best describes the difference between intellectual disabilities and developmental disabilities?

A) Intellectual disabilities strictly impact motor skills, while developmental disabilities only affect cognitive skills.

B) Developmental disabilities always result in a lower IQ, while intellectual disabilities do not.

C) Intellectual disabilities primarily affect cognitive functioning, whereas developmental disabilities may impact multiple areas, including motor skills, language, and behavior.

D) Both terms mean the same thing and are used interchangeably.

Impact of Disabilities on Learning

35. A teacher is working with a student who has a severe disability and struggles with short-term memory retention. What strategy would be most beneficial in supporting their learning?

A) Giving lengthy verbal instructions without written reinforcement

B) Encouraging the student to take responsibility without assistance

C) Using repetition, visual supports, and structured routines

D) Providing unstructured learning experiences to encourage independence

Individualized Learning Needs

36. Which of the following best describes differentiated instruction for students with severe disabilities?

A) Teaching all students the same material in the same way

B) Modifying lessons based on individual student needs and learning styles

C) Providing a single method of assessment for all students

D) Using only verbal instruction without visuals or hands-on activities

Section 2: Planning and Instruction and the Learning Environment

Developing Individualized Education Programs (IEPs)

37. What is a primary benefit of including transition planning in an IEP for students with severe disabilities?

A) It helps students plan for post-school life, including employment, education, and independent living.

B) It focuses only on academic achievement without considering life skills.

C) It ensures that students stay in school indefinitely.

D) It replaces the need for special education services.

Instructional Strategies for Severe to Profound Disabilities

38. Which of the following is the most effective instructional approach for teaching functional skills to students with severe disabilities?

A) Abstract lectures with complex theories

B) Community-based instruction and hands-on learning

C) Only using textbooks for skill development

D) Limiting teaching to classroom-based activities

Classroom and Environmental Modifications

39. Which environmental modification would best support a student with sensory processing difficulties?

A) Using bright flashing lights and loud background noise

B) Creating a structured environment with designated quiet spaces

C) Limiting access to sensory tools such as weighted blankets

D) Allowing unstructured movement throughout the classroom

Behavioral Interventions and Classroom Management

40. What is the primary purpose of Positive Behavioral Interventions and Supports (PBIS) in special education?

A) To provide punishment-based discipline strategies

B) To reinforce positive behaviors and reduce challenging behaviors

C) To rely solely on verbal corrections for misbehavior

D) To remove students with disabilities from the classroom for misbehavior

Section 3: Assessment

Types of Assessments in Special Education

41. Which assessment method provides the most useful information for determining a student's strengths and areas of need in a functional setting?

A) Multiple-choice standardized tests

B) Functional assessments conducted in real-life environments

C) IQ tests with verbal reasoning tasks

D) One-time end-of-year assessments

Assessing Students with Severe to Profound Disabilities

42. A teacher is assessing a student with profound disabilities who has limited verbal communication. What is the most appropriate assessment approach?

A) Require the student to complete a written test

B) Observe the student in multiple settings and use alternative communication methods

C) Only rely on parental reports for assessment

D) Use timed, multiple-choice quizzes

Data Collection and Progress Monitoring

43. Which data collection strategy is most useful for monitoring behavior changes in a student with severe disabilities?

A) Conducting a single observation

B) Using an anecdotal narrative once a semester

C) Implementing frequency and duration recording over time

D) Assessing behavior informally without documentation

Legal and Ethical Considerations in Assessment

44. A special education teacher is administering an assessment to a student with a visual impairment. According to IDEA, what is the teacher's responsibility?

A) Administer the test as-is without modifications

B) Provide an alternative format, such as braille or large print

C) Exclude the student from testing due to the disability

D) Only rely on parent input instead of direct assessment

Section 4: Ethical and Legal Practice, Professionalism, and Collaboration

Special Education Laws and Regulations

45. Which law ensures that individuals with disabilities have the right to reasonable accommodations in educational and workplace settings?

A) Individuals with Disabilities Education Act (IDEA)

B) Americans with Disabilities Act (ADA)

C) Family Educational Rights and Privacy Act (FERPA)

D) No Child Left Behind Act (NCLB)

Ethical Responsibilities in Special Education

46. A teacher notices that a student's IEP accommodations are not being followed by other staff members. What is the most ethical course of action?

A) Ignore the situation since the student is doing well

B) Speak with the responsible staff members and offer support in implementing accommodations

C) Remove all accommodations from the student's plan

D) Inform the student's parents but take no further action

Collaboration with Stakeholders

47. What is the most effective strategy for improving collaboration between special education teachers and families?

A) Limiting communication to annual IEP meetings

B) Using multiple communication methods and involving families in decision-making

C) Keeping parents out of the planning process

D) Providing parents with general education materials only

Advocacy and Professional Development

48. A special education teacher wants to advocate for better resources for students with severe disabilities. What is the most effective action to take?

A) Research current policies and present data-driven proposals to school administrators

B) Ignore the issue and focus only on existing resources

C) Wait for changes to occur without taking action

D) Avoid discussing funding concerns with stakeholders

Section 1: Human Development and Individualized Learning Differences

Theories of Human Development

49. According to Vygotsky's theory of social development, what is the role of scaffolding in learning?

A) It allows students to learn independently without support.
B) It provides structured assistance that is gradually reduced as students gain mastery.
C) It requires students to memorize information without interaction.
D) It discourages peer collaboration in learning.

Understanding Intellectual and Developmental Disabilities (IDD)

50. Which of the following conditions is classified as an intellectual disability rather than a developmental disability?

A) Autism Spectrum Disorder
B) Down Syndrome
C) Cerebral Palsy
D) Sensory Processing Disorder

Impact of Disabilities on Learning

51. A student with a profound disability has difficulty processing verbal information. What is the best instructional strategy for supporting their learning?

A) Speaking at a louder volume
B) Using written-only instruction without visuals
C) Incorporating multi-sensory teaching methods
D) Encouraging the student to learn independently without support

Individualized Learning Needs

52. Which of the following best represents individualized instruction for students with severe disabilities?

A) Using the same curriculum and teaching methods for all students

B) Providing differentiated instruction tailored to each student's needs

C) Limiting instruction to written worksheets

D) Expecting students to self-advocate without support

Section 2: Planning and Instruction and the Learning Environment

Developing Individualized Education Programs (IEPs)

53. What is the primary goal of the Present Levels of Academic Achievement and Functional Performance (PLAAFP) section of an IEP?

A) To determine the student's interests outside of school

B) To describe the student's current academic and functional abilities

C) To assign standardized test scores without considering other factors

D) To set identical learning goals for all students with disabilities

Instructional Strategies for Severe to Profound Disabilities

54. What is an effective way to teach life skills to students with severe disabilities?

A) Providing community-based instruction in real-world settings

B) Relying solely on textbooks and worksheets

C) Expecting students to learn skills without practice

D) Avoiding direct instruction on daily living tasks

Classroom and Environmental Modifications

55. A teacher is designing a classroom for students with severe disabilities. Which modification would best support students with mobility impairments?

A) Providing desks with fixed heights

B) Ensuring that pathways are wide and accessible

C) Arranging furniture without considering wheelchair access

D) Using standard classroom chairs without adjustments

Behavioral Interventions and Classroom Management

56. Which behavioral intervention is most appropriate for a student who engages in frequent self-injurious behaviors?

A) Implementing a Functional Behavior Assessment (FBA) to determine the behavior's function

B) Using only verbal corrections without identifying triggers

C) Ignoring the behavior to see if it stops

D) Restricting all physical movement indefinitely

Section 3: Assessment

Types of Assessments in Special Education

57. What is the primary purpose of dynamic assessment in special education?

A) To measure a student's performance in a single testing session

B) To determine a student's potential for learning with instructional support

C) To compare a student's scores to national averages

D) To assess only academic skills without considering functional abilities

Assessing Students with Severe to Profound Disabilities

58. When assessing students with severe disabilities, what is the best approach to ensure accurate results?

A) Rely only on standardized tests

B) Use a combination of observations, caregiver input, and alternative assessments

C) Ignore behavior and focus only on written tests

D) Assess in a stressful environment to challenge the student

Data Collection and Progress Monitoring

59. A teacher is tracking a student's progress on an IEP goal related to communication. Which data collection method is most effective?

A) Randomly observing the student without taking notes

B) Keeping detailed records using frequency counts and anecdotal logs

C) Only reviewing progress at annual IEP meetings

D) Using the same assessment method for all students

Legal and Ethical Considerations in Assessment

60. A special education teacher is administering an assessment to a student with an expressive language disorder. What is the teacher's legal obligation?

A) Administer the test without accommodations

B) Use alternative assessment methods that do not require verbal responses

C) Modify the test without informing the IEP team

D) Refuse to assess the student due to their communication difficulties

Section 4: Ethical and Legal Practice, Professionalism, and Collaboration

Special Education Laws and Regulations

61. Under the Individuals with Disabilities Education Act (IDEA), how often must an Individualized Education Program (IEP) be reviewed?

A) Every five years

B) Once every three years

C) Annually, or more often if needed

D) Only if the parents request a review

Ethical Responsibilities in Special Education

62. A teacher learns that a student's IEP services are not being provided as required. What is the most ethical response?

A) Ignore the issue and continue teaching

B) Document concerns and report them to the appropriate personnel

C) Remove the student from general education classes

D) Tell the student's parents that nothing can be done

Collaboration with Stakeholders

63. A special education teacher is planning a meeting with a student's general education teacher and parents. What is the best way to ensure a productive discussion?

A) Allow only the school staff to make decisions

B) Encourage open communication and collaborative problem-solving

C) Avoid discussing challenges to keep the meeting positive

D) Exclude the general education teacher from the discussion

Advocacy and Professional Development

64. A teacher wants to stay current on best practices for educating students with severe disabilities. Which professional development activity would be most beneficial?

A) Attending special education workshops and conferences

B) Using only personal teaching experiences for professional growth

C) Avoiding new research due to time constraints

D) Continuing to use outdated methods without updates

Section 1: Human Development and Individualized Learning Differences

Theories of Human Development

65. Which of the following best represents a key principle of Bronfenbrenner's Ecological Systems Theory in relation to special education?

A) Development occurs only through genetic predisposition.

B) A child's development is influenced by multiple environmental systems, including family, school, and community.

C) Intelligence is fixed at birth and cannot be changed by external influences.

D) Only direct caregivers impact a child's growth and learning.

Understanding Intellectual and Developmental Disabilities (IDD)

66. Which of the following is a primary characteristic of Fragile X Syndrome, a developmental disability?

A) Significant vision loss

B) Impaired social communication and repetitive behaviors

C) Unusual flexibility and joint hypermobility

D) Difficulty swallowing and frequent choking episodes

Impact of Disabilities on Learning

67. How does an auditory processing disorder (APD) impact a student's learning experience?

A) The student has difficulty with physical coordination.

B) The student struggles with understanding spoken language despite normal hearing ability.

C) The student experiences severe vision impairments.

D) The student has difficulty regulating emotions and behavior.

Individualized Learning Needs

68. Which instructional approach is best suited for a student with severe cognitive disabilities who learns best through repetition?

A) Inquiry-based learning without structured guidance

B) Scaffolded instruction with consistent reinforcement

C) Lecture-based instruction with minimal teacher interaction

D) Self-directed learning with no modifications

Section 2: Planning and Instruction and the Learning Environment

Developing Individualized Education Programs (IEPs)

69. In an IEP meeting, what is the best way to ensure that goals are measurable and achievable?

A) Writing vague goals to allow flexibility in interpretation

B) Using SMART criteria (Specific, Measurable, Achievable, Relevant, Time-bound)

C) Setting goals based only on what the general education teacher recommends

D) Focusing only on behavioral goals rather than academic progress

Instructional Strategies for Severe to Profound Disabilities

70. Which of the following is an example of augmentative and alternative communication (AAC) that can help a nonverbal student communicate?

A) A student learns sign language or uses a picture communication board.

B) The teacher relies solely on verbal communication without additional tools.

C) The student is required to communicate only through writing.

D) The student is expected to learn to speak before being given communication support.

Classroom and Environmental Modifications

71. What is the main purpose of a sensory break for students with severe disabilities?

A) To discipline students for misbehavior
B) To provide opportunities for sensory regulation and self-regulation
C) To limit participation in classroom activities
D) To replace academic instruction

Behavioral Interventions and Classroom Management

72. A student with severe autism exhibits hand-flapping behaviors. Which strategy would be most effective in addressing this behavior?

A) Ignoring the behavior completely
B) Punishing the student to discourage hand-flapping
C) Identifying the function of the behavior and providing alternative sensory input
D) Restricting the student's movement entirely

Section 3: Assessment

Types of Assessments in Special Education

73. Which type of assessment is best suited to measure a student's ability to complete life skills tasks independently?

A) Standardized multiple-choice test
B) Functional skills checklist and observational assessment

C) IQ test

D) High-stakes written exam

Assessing Students with Severe to Profound Disabilities

74. What is the best approach to assess a student with a profound intellectual disability who has limited verbal and motor abilities?

A) Use multiple-choice exams without accommodations

B) Observe the student's interactions and responses to stimuli

C) Rely only on parent-reported data

D) Assess the student only once per year

Data Collection and Progress Monitoring

75. A teacher is tracking a student's progress in using an adaptive communication device. What is the best method for monitoring this skill?

A) Reviewing progress once every six months

B) Recording the number of successful communication attempts daily

C) Relying only on verbal teacher reports

D) Only tracking incorrect responses

Legal and Ethical Considerations in Assessment

76. According to IDEA, which factor must be considered when selecting an assessment for a student with disabilities?

A) The assessment should be given in the student's primary language and mode of communication

B) The test must be the same as that given to general education students

C) No accommodations should be provided to ensure fairness

D) The assessment should only focus on academic abilities

Section 4: Ethical and Legal Practice, Professionalism, and Collaboration

Special Education Laws and Regulations

77. Which law requires that students with disabilities have access to education in the least restrictive environment (LRE)?

A) Every Student Succeeds Act (ESSA)

B) Individuals with Disabilities Education Act (IDEA)

C) Americans with Disabilities Act (ADA)

D) Family Educational Rights and Privacy Act (FERPA)

Ethical Responsibilities in Special Education

78. If a special education teacher believes that a student's current placement does not meet their needs, what is the most ethical course of action?

A) Make the decision independently and remove the student from the current setting

B) Discuss concerns with the IEP team and parents to determine appropriate changes

C) Ignore the issue since placement decisions are final

D) Advise the parents to withdraw the student from school

Collaboration with Stakeholders

79. A general education teacher expresses concern about including a student with severe disabilities in their classroom. What is the best way for the special education teacher to respond?

A) Offer professional development and co-planning strategies for effective inclusion

B) Suggest removing the student from the classroom

C) Ignore the concern and allow the teacher to manage independently

D) Encourage the teacher to use the same methods as with other students

Advocacy and Professional Development

80. What is one of the most effective ways for a special education teacher to advocate for students with severe disabilities?

A) Attending professional development workshops and advocating for evidence-based practices

B) Avoiding discussions about policy changes

C) Limiting interactions with school administration

D) Keeping concerns about student rights private

Section 1: Human Development and Individualized Learning Differences

Theories of Human Development

81. According to Piaget's stages of cognitive development, which stage is characterized by the ability to think abstractly and reason logically?

A) Sensorimotor

B) Preoperational

C) Concrete Operational

D) Formal Operational

Understanding Intellectual and Developmental Disabilities (IDD)

82. Which of the following is a common characteristic of individuals with severe intellectual disabilities?

A) Advanced problem-solving skills

B) Difficulty with adaptive behaviors and independent living skills

C) Strong verbal communication abilities

D) Rapid skill acquisition across multiple domains

Impact of Disabilities on Learning

83. How does cerebral palsy (CP) primarily affect a student's ability to learn in a classroom setting?

A) It only affects cognitive abilities and memory.

B) It primarily impacts muscle control, coordination, and mobility.

C) It always results in intellectual disabilities.

D) It causes severe emotional disturbances.

Individualized Learning Needs

84. A student with a severe disability has difficulty transitioning between tasks. What is the most effective strategy to support them?

A) Verbal instructions without any visual supports

B) Using a visual schedule and transition cues

C) Changing activities without warning to encourage adaptability

D) Limiting classroom activities to one subject

Section 2: Planning and Instruction and the Learning Environment

Developing Individualized Education Programs (IEPs)

85. In an IEP, what is the purpose of the accommodations section?

A) To set strict limits on a student's participation in general education

B) To outline modifications to the curriculum

C) To describe supports that help the student access learning without changing learning expectations

D) To document only the student's weaknesses

Instructional Strategies for Severe to Profound Disabilities

86. What is the primary advantage of using task analysis when teaching students with severe disabilities?

A) It simplifies learning by breaking down complex tasks into smaller, manageable steps.

B) It eliminates the need for reinforcement.

C) It requires students to learn skills independently.

D) It relies solely on auditory instruction.

Classroom and Environmental Modifications

87. Which of the following classroom modifications would best support a student with sensory processing challenges?

A) Bright flashing lights and loud background noise

B) A structured environment with sensory-friendly spaces

C) A classroom with unpredictable schedules and frequent disruptions

D) A single method of instruction with no visual aids

Behavioral Interventions and Classroom Management

88. What is the best approach for reducing aggressive behaviors in a student with severe disabilities?

A) Implementing a Functional Behavior Assessment (FB A) to determine the cause

B) Using punishment-based strategies

C) Ignoring the behavior until it stops

D) Removing the student from the classroom permanently

Section 3: Assessment

Types of Assessments in Special Education

89. Which of the following assessment tools is best suited for evaluating the communication abilities of a nonverbal student with severe disabilities?

A) Standardized reading comprehension test

B) Augmentative and Alternative Communication (AAC) evaluation

C) Timed multiple-choice exam

D) Traditional IQ test

Assessing Students with Severe to Profound Disabilities

90. A teacher wants to assess a student's ability to follow daily routines independently. Which assessment method would be most effective?

A) A multiple-choice test on daily living skills

B) Observational assessment in natural settings

C) A written essay about routines

D) A standardized intelligence test

Data Collection and Progress Monitoring

91. What is the primary benefit of using a data collection system in special education?

A) It provides an objective way to track student progress and guide instruction.

B) It only documents negative behaviors for discipline purposes.

C) It is used exclusively for legal purposes.

D) It replaces the need for direct observation.

Legal and Ethical Considerations in Assessment

92. Which principle must be followed when administering assessments to students with disabilities under IDEA?

A) The test must be given in a standardized format with no modifications.

B) The assessment must be tailored to the student's communication and learning needs.

C) The student must take the same test as general education students.

D) The results must only be used for disciplinary purposes.

Section 4: Ethical and Legal Practice, Professionalism, and Collaboration

Special Education Laws and Regulations

93. Under the Americans with Disabilities Act (AD A), which of the following must public schools provide for students with disabilities?

A) Equal access to educational programs and reasonable accommodations

B) Private tutoring for all students with disabilities

C) Free college tuition

D) Separate classrooms for all students with disabilities

Ethical Responsibilities in Special Education

94. If a teacher observes that a student with an IEP is not receiving their legally mandated accommodations, what should they do?

A) Ignore the issue unless the parents complain

B) Advocate for the student by reporting the issue to the IEP team and school administration

C) Remove the student from general education classes

D) Reduce the student's workload to compensate for the lack of accommodations

Collaboration with Stakeholders

95. Which of the following strategies is most effective for fostering collaboration between parents and special education teachers?

A) Communicating only during annual IEP meetings

B) Providing regular updates and involving parents in decision-making

C) Limiting parent involvement to academic subjects only

D) Only sharing positive feedback and avoiding discussions of challenges

Advocacy and Professional Development

96. What is an effective way for special education teachers to stay updated on best practices?

A) Attending professional development workshops and conferences

B) Relying only on personal classroom experience

C) Avoiding collaboration with other educators

D) Using outdated instructional methods

Section 1: Human Development and Individualized Learning Differences

Theories of Human Development

97. According to Maslow's hierarchy of needs, which of the following must be met before a student can achieve higher-level learning?

A) Self-actualization

B) Safety and physiological needs

C) Creative problem-solving

D) Mastery of academic subjects

Understanding Intellectual and Developmental Disabilities (IDD)

98. A student with Down syndrome often struggles with short-term memory retention. Which strategy would be most effective in supporting their learning?

A) Presenting information only once without review

B) Using visual aids, repetition, and structured practice

C) Encouraging self-teaching without support

D) Limiting the student's participation in activities

Impact of Disabilities on Learning

99. Which of the following is a common challenge faced by students with profound intellectual disabilities?

A) Strong independent problem-solving skills

B) Limited ability to generalize learned skills across different settings

C) Fast-paced language comprehension and expression

D) Mastery of abstract mathematical concepts without support

Individualized Learning Needs

100. A teacher is developing an instructional plan for a student with a severe intellectual disability. What is the most important factor to consider?

A) The student should be expected to learn at the same pace as their peers.

B) The instruction should be highly individualized and focused on functional skills.

C) The curriculum should be identical to that of general education students without modifications.

D) The student should only receive academic instruction, with no focus on life skills.

5.2 ANSWER SHEET - PRACTICE TEST 1

1. Answer: B) Learning is a social process, and children develop through interactions with more knowledgeable others.

Explanation: Lev Vygotsky's **Zone of Proximal Development (ZPD)** suggests that children learn best through **social interaction and guided support** from more capable peers or adults. This theory is especially relevant in **special education**, where **scaffolding and individualized support** are crucial for student learning and development.

2. Answer: C) They often require significant support in daily living skills.

Explanation: Students with severe to profound intellectual disabilities often struggle with **adaptive behaviors**, including communication, self-care, and social skills. They require **extensive individualized support** in both **academic and daily living activities**.

3. Answer: C) The presence of co-occurring medical conditions

Explanation: Many students with **severe to profound disabilities** also have **co-occurring medical conditions** such as epilepsy, cerebral palsy, or sensory impairments, which can greatly impact **learning, mobility, communication, and endurance in classroom activities**.

4. Answer: B) Task analysis and systematic instruction tailored to each student

Explanation: Task analysis involves breaking down skills into **smaller, manageable steps**, which helps **students with severe disabilities learn effectively**. **Systematic instruction** ensures that learning is structured, repetitive, and tailored to individual needs, leading to greater success in mastering skills.

5. Answer: B) To set individualized goals and outline services for students with disabilities

Explanation: An **IEP is a legally binding document** that outlines the **specific educational goals, services, and accommodations** a student with disabilities needs to succeed in school. It is **developed collaboratively** by educators, specialists, and parents.

6. Answer: B) The use of Augmentative and Alternative Communication (AAC) devices

Explanation: Many students with **severe disabilities are nonverbal or have limited verbal skills. AAC devices**, such as **speech-generating devices, picture exchange systems, and communication boards**, provide alternative ways for students to express their needs and participate in learning.

7. Answer: B) Providing a structured, predictable environment with clear visual schedules

Explanation: Students with severe disabilities thrive in structured, predictable environments. Visual schedules, sensory-friendly spaces, and adaptive equipment help **reduce anxiety and enhance engagement** in the learning process.

8. Answer: B) Conducting a Functional Behavior Assessment (FBA) to identify triggers

Explanation: An **FBA** helps determine the cause **(antecedents and consequences) of a student's challenging behaviors.** Once triggers are identified, **individualized behavioral interventions can be implemented** to teach alternative, appropriate behaviors.

9. Answer: B) Functional and curriculum-based assessments

Explanation: Functional and curriculum-based assessments focus on measuring a student's ability to perform **daily living, communication, and academic tasks in real-world settings.** These assessments provide meaningful insights for students with **severe disabilities who may not perform well on traditional standardized tests.**

10. Answer: B) Direct observation and performance-based assessments

Explanation: For nonverbal students, assessments should focus on direct observation, performance tasks, and alternative communication methods. Teachers should evaluate a student's ability to **engage with tasks, use assistive technology, and respond to stimuli in an adapted environment.**

11. Answer: B) Systematic data collection using checklists, graphs, and anecdotal records

Explanation: Consistently tracking student progress using **data collection tools** (e.g., **checklists, frequency counts, and progress graphs**) helps educators **monitor learning, make instructional adjustments, and support data-driven decision-making for IEP goals.**

12. Answer: A) In a language and format the student understands

Explanation: IDEA requires assessments to be nondiscriminatory and conducted in the student's primary language or communication mode to ensure **fair and accurate results**. This law promotes **equity in assessment** for students with disabilities.

13. Answer: C) Individuals with Disabilities Education Act (IDEA)

Explanation: IDEA guarantees that students with disabilities receive Free Appropriate Public Education (FAPE) in the Least Restrictive Environment (LRE). This ensures **equal access to education with necessary supports and services**.

14. Answer: C) Discuss concerns with the colleague and collaborate to ensure compliance

Explanation: Special education professionals have an ethical obligation to advocate for students and ensure that their educational plans are followed. Addressing concerns professionally and collaborating with colleagues **helps protect student rights and maintain ethical standards**.

15. Answer: B) Holding regular co-planning meetings to align instructional strategies

Explanation: Effective collaboration requires special and general education teachers to work together regularly to modify lessons, provide accommodations, and ensure that **students with disabilities receive appropriate support in inclusive settings**.

16. Answer: A) Attending special education conferences and workshops

Explanation: Ongoing professional development through **conferences, workshops, online training, and peer collaboration** helps educators **stay current with best practices, new research, and legal updates in special education**.

17. Answer: C) Concrete Operational Stage

Explanation: Piaget's **Concrete Operational Stage (ages 7-11)** is when children develop **logical thinking about concrete objects** but struggle with **abstract reasoning**. This stage is important in **special education, as students with intellectual disabilities may require hands-on learning methods.**

18. Answer: B) Limited ability to generalize learned skills to new settings

Explanation: Students with severe intellectual disabilities often struggle to transfer skills from one context to another, requiring **explicit instruction, real-life practice, and repeated exposure** to concepts in various settings.

19. Answer: B) Using short, structured activities with frequent breaks

Explanation: Students with severe disabilities benefit from structured, engaging activities with built-in breaks to maintain attention. Strategies such as **visual cues, hands-on activities, and sensory breaks** help sustain focus and improve learning outcomes.

20. Answer: B) Personalized learning plans based on student strengths and needs

Explanation: Individualized instruction ensures that lessons are tailored to a student's cognitive, communicative, and sensory abilities. Approaches such as **differentiation, assistive technology, and hands-on learning** help optimize student success.

21. Answer: B) Specific, measurable, achievable, relevant, and time-bound (SMART) criteria

Explanation: IEP goals should follow the SMART format to ensure clear expectations and measurable progress. For example, instead of saying "John will improve reading," a SMART goal would be: **"John will identify 10 sight words with 80% accuracy within 6 months using visual aids."**

22. Answer: B) Break down the skill into small, sequential steps

Explanation: Task analysis involves breaking complex skills into smaller, manageable steps so that students can learn systematically. For handwashing, steps may include **turning on water, applying soap, scrubbing hands, rinsing, and drying**.

23. Answer: B) They help students understand and anticipate daily routines

Explanation: Visual schedules provide structure and predictability, reducing anxiety and supporting independence in students with severe disabilities. These schedules use **pictures, symbols, or written cues** to help students transition between tasks smoothly.

24. Answer: B) Providing alternative, functionally equivalent replacement behaviors

Explanation: Self-stimulatory behaviors serve a purpose for the student, such as self-regulation or sensory input. Providing **alternative strategies** (e.g., fidget toys, movement breaks, deep-pressure activities) helps meet the student's needs in an appropriate manner.

25. Answer: B) Curriculum-based assessments (CBAs)

Explanation: CBAs are tailored to measure student progress on specific learning objectives, making them the best tool for monitoring IEP goal attainment. They provide direct feedback and guide instruction based on the student's needs.

26. Answer: B) Using adaptive communication tools and structured observations

Explanation: Assessing nonverbal students requires the use of Augmentative and Alternative Communication (AAC) tools, structured observa-

tions, and real-life performance assessments. This ensures that the student's full abilities are accurately measured.

27. Answer: B) Using a frequency recording chart to document progress daily

Explanation: Daily tracking through frequency recording helps educators identify patterns, determine effectiveness of interventions, and make timely instructional adjustments. Consistent data collection ensures meaningful progress monitoring.

28. Answer: B) In the student's primary language or communication mode

Explanation: IDEA mandates that assessments be administered in a way that does not disadvantage students due to language or communication barriers. This ensures **fair and accurate representation of the student's abilities.**

29. Answer: B) To ensure that students with disabilities are educated alongside peers to the greatest extent possible

Explanation: LRE ensures that students with disabilities receive their education in the most inclusive setting possible, with appropriate support and accommodations. This allows them to interact with typically developing peers while receiving necessary specialized instruction.

30. Answer: B) Ensuring that the family fully understands the IEP and their rights

Explanation: Teachers must ensure that parents/guardians understand the IEP, their rights, and available support services. Transparency and collaboration are essential ethical responsibilities in special education.

31. Answer: B) Regularly co-planning lessons and sharing resources

Explanation: Collaboration between special and general education teachers enhances inclusive education. Regular co-planning ensures **consistent support, differentiation, and proper implementation of accommodations for students with disabilities.**

32. Answer: A) Attending professional development workshops and conferences

Explanation: Continuous learning through workshops, conferences, and professional organizations ensures that teachers stay up to date with **best practices, legal changes, and innovative strategies in special education.**

33. Answer: C) Forming identity vs. role confusion

Explanation: Erikson's stage of "Identity vs. Role Confusion" (adolescence) focuses on self-identity and personal values. Adolescents with disabilities may require additional support in **self-advocacy, confidence building, and career planning** to navigate this stage successfully.

34. Answer: C) Intellectual disabilities primarily affect cognitive functioning, whereas developmental disabilities may impact multiple areas, including motor skills, language, and behavior.

Explanation: Intellectual disabilities involve significant cognitive impairments that impact reasoning and problem-solving. Developmental disabilities, such as **autism spectrum disorder and cerebral palsy,** may include **motor, sensory, and communication difficulties in addition to cognitive challenges.**

35. Answer: C) Using repetition, visual supports, and structured routines

Explanation: Students with memory deficits benefit from structured repetition, visuals, and predictable routines. These strategies reinforce learning and **help transfer skills to long-term memory.**

36. Answer: B) Modifying lessons based on individual student needs and learning styles

Explanation: Differentiated instruction involves adjusting teaching methods, content, and assessment strategies to **meet diverse student needs.** This is crucial for students with **severe disabilities who require individualized support.**

37. Answer: A) It helps students plan for post-school life, including employment, education, and independent living.

Explanation: Transition planning, required by IDEA, ensures that students with disabilities receive support for future independence, career opportunities, and community participation.

38. Answer: B) Community-based instruction and hands-on learning

Explanation: Students with severe disabilities benefit from real-world, hands-on learning experiences, such as practicing grocery shopping, meal preparation, and self-care tasks.

39. Answer: B) Creating a structured environment with designated quiet spaces

Explanation: Providing sensory-friendly spaces, visual schedules, and calming areas helps students with sensory processing difficulties remain **focused and regulated** in the classroom.

40. Answer: B) To reinforce positive behaviors and reduce challenging behaviors

Explanation: PBIS focuses on proactive strategies such as positive reinforcement, structured routines, and individualized interventions to help students develop appropriate behaviors.

41. Answer: B) Functional assessments conducted in real-life environments

Explanation: Functional assessments measure how well a student performs everyday tasks, such as dressing, meal preparation, and communication, in real-world settings. These assessments provide **practical insights** into student capabilities and needed support.

42. Answer: B) Observe the student in multiple settings and use alternative communication methods

Explanation: Students with profound disabilities require assessments that consider alternative communication methods and real-life performance. Observations, **AAC devices, and caregiver input** help provide a more accurate picture of a student's skills.

43. Answer: C) Implementing frequency and duration recording over time

Explanation: Tracking behavior patterns over time using systematic data collection methods such as frequency, duration, and antecedent-behavior-consequence (ABC) charts provides measurable insights for intervention planning.

44. Answer: B) Provide an alternative format, such as braille or large print

Explanation: IDEA mandates that assessments be administered in a way that accommodates a student's disability, ensuring fair and accurate measurement of their abilities. Providing braille, large print, or verbal formats supports accessibility.

45. Answer: B) Americans with Disabilities Act (ADA)

Explanation: The ADA protects individuals with disabilities from discrimination and requires reasonable accommodations in schools, workplaces, and public spaces.

46. Answer: B) Speak with the responsible staff members and offer support in implementing accommodations

Explanation: Special education teachers must advocate for students by ensuring that IEP accommodations are properly implemented to meet legal and ethical obligations.

47. Answer: B) Using multiple communication methods and involving families in decision-making

Explanation: Building strong partnerships with families through consistent communication (meetings, emails, home visits, phone calls) leads to better student outcomes. Involving parents in **goal-setting and interventions** enhances support.

48. Answer: A) Research current policies and present data-driven proposals to school administrators

Explanation: Advocacy in special education requires using research, data, and collaboration with stakeholders to push for improvements in resources, training, and services for students with disabilities.

49. Answer: B) It provides structured assistance that is gradually reduced as students gain mastery.

Explanation: Scaffolding refers to providing temporary support to help students reach higher levels of understanding. The support is gradually removed as students **develop independent problem-solving skills.**

50. Answer: B) Down Syndrome

Explanation: Down Syndrome is an intellectual disability characterized by cognitive impairments, whereas conditions like cerebral palsy and autism spectrum disorder primarily affect motor, communication, or behavioral skills.

51. Answer: C) Incorporating multi-sensory teaching methods

Explanation: **Students with processing difficulties benefit from multi-sensory approaches, including visual supports, hands-on activities, and auditory cues.** These strategies enhance comprehension and retention.

52. Answer: B) Providing differentiated instruction tailored to each student's needs

Explanation: **Individualized instruction involves adapting teaching methods, pacing, and materials based on a student's strengths and needs.** This ensures equitable access to learning opportunities.

53. Answer: B) To describe the student's current academic and functional abilities

Explanation: **The PLAAFP section outlines a student's strengths, weaknesses, and areas for growth.** This information helps create **realistic, measurable IEP goals.**

54. Answer: A) Providing community-based instruction in real-world settings

Explanation: **Community-based instruction (CBI) allows students to practice skills in real environments, such as grocery stores, workplaces, or public transportation.** This helps students develop independence.

55. Answer: B) Ensuring that pathways are wide and accessible

Explanation: An accessible classroom includes wide pathways, adjustable desks, and adaptive seating to accommodate students with mobility impairments.

56. Answer: A) Implementing a Functional Behavior Assessment (FBA) to determine the behavior's function

Explanation: An FBA helps identify why a behavior occurs (e.g., sensory needs, escape, attention-seeking) and leads to an appropriate, evidence-based intervention plan.

57. Answer: B) To determine a student's potential for learning with instructional support

Explanation: Dynamic assessment evaluates how a student learns with guidance, rather than just measuring static ability. It is useful for students with severe disabilities to determine the best instructional approaches.

58. Answer: B) Use a combination of observations, caregiver input, and alternative assessments

Explanation: A holistic approach, including direct observation, input from caregivers, and functional performance assessments, provides a more accurate picture of a student's abilities.

59. Answer: B) Keeping detailed records using frequency counts and anecdotal logs

Explanation: Systematic data collection ensures that progress is accurately documented, allowing for instructional adjustments when needed.

60. Answer: B) Use alternative assessment methods that do not require verbal responses

Explanation: Students with communication challenges must be provided with alternative ways to demonstrate their knowledge, such as using assistive technology or written responses.

61. Answer: C) Annually, or more often if needed

Explanation: IEPs must be reviewed at least once a year to assess progress and make necessary updates. Additional reviews can occur if parents or educators identify a need for changes.

62. Answer: B) Document concerns and report them to the appropriate personnel

Explanation: Teachers have an ethical responsibility to advocate for their students and ensure that IEP services are fully implemented as required by law.

63. Answer: B) Encourage open communication and collaborative problem-solving

Explanation: Effective collaboration between teachers and parents ensures that students receive appropriate support and that decisions are made with all stakeholders involved.

64. Answer: A) Attending special education workshops and conferences

Explanation: Engaging in professional development ensures that teachers remain knowledgeable about new strategies, laws, and best practices in special education.

65. Answer: B) A child's development is influenced by multiple environmental systems, including family, school, and community.

Explanation: Bronfenbrenner's Ecological Systems Theory emphasizes that a child's development is shaped by different environmental layers (microsystem, mesosystem, exosystem, macrosystem), which include **family, peers, school, and broader societal factors.**

66. Answer: B) Impaired social communication and repetitive behaviors

Explanation: Fragile X Syndrome is a genetic condition often associated with intellectual disability, anxiety, social challenges, and repetitive behaviors, similar to characteristics seen in autism spectrum disorder.

67. Answer: B) The student struggles with understanding spoken language despite normal hearing ability.

Explanation: Students with APD have difficulty distinguishing and processing sounds, which affects their ability to follow directions, understand speech, and engage in verbal learning.

68. Answer: B) Scaffolded instruction with consistent reinforcement

Explanation: Students with severe cognitive disabilities benefit from scaffolded instruction, where tasks are broken into smaller steps, reinforced consistently, and gradually removed as students gain independence.

69. Answer: B) Using SMART criteria (Specific, Measurable, Achievable, Relevant, Time-bound)

Explanation: SMART goals ensure that a student's progress can be tracked objectively, allowing educators and parents to measure success and adjust strategies when needed.

70. Answer: A) A student learns sign language or uses a picture communication board.

Explanation: AAC includes tools like sign language, picture exchange communication systems (PECS), and speech-generating devices that support students with limited verbal abilities.

71. Answer: B) To provide opportunities for sensory regulation and self-regulation

Explanation: Sensory breaks help students who experience sensory processing challenges regulate their emotions, focus better, and participate more effectively in learning activities.

72. Answer: C) Identifying the function of the behavior and providing alternative sensory input

Explanation: Hand-flapping is often a self-stimulatory (stimming) behavior. Providing an alternative sensory activity, such as using fidget toys or deep-pressure input, can help the student regulate their needs in an appropriate way.

73. Answer: B) Functional skills checklist and observational assessment

Explanation: Functional assessments focus on how well students perform everyday activities, such as dressing, cooking, and managing personal hygiene, rather than academic abilities.

74. Answer: B) Observe the student's interactions and responses to stimuli

Explanation: Observational assessments provide insights into how students communicate, process information, and engage with their environment when traditional assessments are not appropriate.

75. Answer: B) Recording the number of successful communication attempts daily

Explanation: Regular data collection ensures that progress is monitored accurately and that adjustments can be made to improve the student's communication skills.

76. Answer: A) The assessment should be given in the student's primary language and mode of communication

Explanation: IDEA requires that assessments be accessible to students by using their preferred communication methods, ensuring that their abilities are accurately measured.

77. Answer: B) Individuals with Disabilities Education Act (IDEA)

Explanation: IDEA mandates that students with disabilities be placed in the least restrictive environment (LRE), meaning they should be educated alongside peers without disabilities to the greatest extent possible.

78. Answer: B) Discuss concerns with the IEP team and parents to determine appropriate changes

Explanation: Placement decisions should be made collaboratively with the IEP team, considering the student's best interests and legal requirements.

79. Answer: A) Offer professional development and co-planning strategies for effective inclusion

Explanation: Supporting general education teachers through training, co-teaching, and instructional strategies helps ensure successful inclusion and better student outcomes.

80. Answer: A) Attending professional development workshops and advocating for evidence-based practices

Explanation: Advocacy includes staying informed on best practices, engaging in policy discussions, and ensuring that students receive appropriate supports and services.

81. Answer: D) Formal Operational

Explanation: The Formal Operational stage (ages 12 and up) is when individuals develop the ability to think abstractly, reason logically, and solve hypothetical problems. However, students with severe disabilities may require **additional support to develop higher-order thinking skills.**

82. Answer: B) Difficulty with adaptive behaviors and independent living skills

Explanation: Individuals with severe intellectual disabilities often require support with adaptive skills, such as self-care, communication, and independent living. These challenges affect their ability to function in everyday life without assistance.

83. Answer: B) It primarily impacts muscle control, coordination, and mobility.

Explanation: Cerebral palsy is a motor disorder that affects movement and muscle tone. While some individuals with CP have intellectual disabilities, many have normal cognitive abilities but require assistive technology and physical accommodations.

84. Answer: B) Using a visual schedule and transition cues

Explanation: Students with severe disabilities often benefit from structured routines, visual schedules, and transition warnings (such as timers or verbal cues) to help them prepare for changes in activities.

85. Answer: C) To describe supports that help the student access learning without changing learning expectations

Explanation: Accommodations provide support (such as extended time, assistive technology, or a quiet testing environment) without altering academic expectations. Modifications, on the other hand, **change the content or learning goals.**

86. Answer: A) It simplifies learning by breaking down complex tasks into smaller, manageable steps.

Explanation: Task analysis helps students learn complex skills by teaching each step individually before combining them into a complete sequence. This approach is especially useful for teaching daily living and vocational skills.

87. Answer: B) A structured environment with sensory-friendly spaces

Explanation: Students with sensory processing challenges often benefit from structured environments, predictable routines, and sensory breaks to help them self-regulate.

88. Answer: A) Implementing a Functional Behavior Assessment (FBA) to determine the cause

Explanation: An FBA identifies triggers and functions of challenging behaviors, allowing educators to develop effective interventions that replace aggressive behaviors with appropriate alternatives.

89. Answer: B) Augmentative and Alternative Communication (AAC) evaluation

Explanation: An AAC evaluation determines the best communication tools (e.g., speech-generating devices, picture boards) for students who are nonverbal or have limited speech abilities.

90. Answer: B) Observational assessment in natural settings

Explanation: Observing a student in real-life settings (e.g., classroom, home, community) provides valuable information on their ability to perform tasks independently.

91. Answer: A) It provides an objective way to track student progress and guide instruction.

Explanation: Data collection helps educators monitor student progress, adjust instructional strategies, and ensure that interventions are effective.

92. Answer: B) The assessment must be tailored to the student's communication and learning needs.

Explanation: IDEA requires that assessments be adapted (e.g., braille, sign language, assistive technology) to ensure accurate measurement of a student's abilities.

93. Answer: A) Equal access to educational programs and reasonable accommodations

Explanation: The ADA ensures that students with disabilities receive reasonable accommodations and have equal opportunities in education, employment, and public services.

94. Answer: B) Advocate for the student by reporting the issue to the IEP team and school administration

Explanation: Special education teachers must ensure that students receive the services outlined in their IEP and advocate for necessary accommodations.

95. Answer: B) Providing regular updates and involving parents in decision-making

Explanation: Strong collaboration between teachers and parents leads to better educational outcomes by ensuring consistency in learning strategies and support across home and school environments.

96. Answer: A) Attending professional development workshops and conferences

Explanation: Continuing education through professional development helps teachers stay informed on new strategies, laws, and best practices in special education.

97. Answer: B) Safety and physiological needs

Explanation: Maslow's hierarchy of needs suggests that basic needs (such as food, shelter, and safety) must be met before a student can focus on higher-order skills like problem-solving and academic achievement.

98. Answer: B) Using visual aids, repetition, and structured practice

Explanation: Students with Down syndrome often benefit from repeated practice, visual supports, and structured learning approaches to reinforce memory and comprehension.

99. Answer: B) Limited ability to generalize learned skills across different settings

Explanation: Students with profound intellectual disabilities often struggle to apply skills learned in one context to new situations. Instruction should include multiple settings and consistent reinforcement to support generalization.

100. Answer: B) The instruction should be highly individualized and focused on functional skills.

Explanation: Instruction for students with severe disabilities should be tailored to their specific needs, emphasizing practical, functional skills that support independence and daily living.

6.1 FULL-LENGTH PRACTICE TEST 2

Section 1: Human Development and Individualized Learning Differences

Theories of Human Development

101. According to Erikson's psychosocial theory, which developmental stage is most critical for establishing a sense of independence in early childhood?

A) Trust vs. Mistrust

B) Autonomy vs. Shame and Doubt

C) Initiative vs. Guilt

D) Industry vs. Inferiority

Understanding Intellectual and Developmental Disabilities (IDD)

102. Which of the following is a hallmark characteristic of Prader-Willi Syndrome, a developmental disability?

A) Excessive appetite and food-seeking behavior

B) Severe visual impairment

C) Loss of hearing in both ears

D) Uncontrolled muscle spasms

Impact of Disabilities on Learning

103. A student with a severe disability struggles with processing spoken instructions. What strategy would be most beneficial?

A) Speaking faster to encourage attention

B) Providing written and visual instructions along with verbal cues

C) Limiting instruction to one mode of communication

D) Relying only on peer assistance for comprehension

Individualized Learning Needs

104. When planning instruction for a student with profound intellectual disabilities, what is the most important factor?

A) The student's ability to perform at grade level

B) The student's individualized learning style and needs

C) The average skill level of their classmates

D) The student's ability to take standardized tests

Section 2: Planning and Instruction and the Learning Environment

Developing Individualized Education Programs (IEPs)

105. Which of the following is a required component of an Individualized Education Program (IEP)?

A) The student's height and weight

B) A list of every assignment the student will complete

C) Measurable annual goals based on the student's present levels of performance

D) A statement prohibiting changes to the IEP

Instructional Strategies for Severe to Profound Disabilities

106. Which instructional strategy is most effective for teaching a student with limited verbal communication?

A) Lecturing without using visuals

B) Encouraging the use of Augmentative and Alternative Communication (AAC) devices

C) Avoiding nonverbal communication methods

D) Using only written text without speech support

Classroom and Environmental Modifications

107. What is an essential feature of a well-designed classroom for students with severe disabilities?

A) Unstructured seating and unpredictable schedules

B) A structured, predictable environment with accessible materials

C) Bright, flashing lights to keep students alert

D) Loud background noise to encourage attention

Behavioral Interventions and Classroom Management

108. Which positive behavioral intervention is most effective for a student who frequently engages in self-injurious behaviors?

A) Ignoring the behavior until it stops

B) Providing alternative behaviors that fulfill the same function

C) Using punishment-based methods only

D) Removing the student from the classroom permanently

Section 3: Assessment

Types of Assessments in Special Education

109. Which type of assessment is best suited for tracking small increments of progress in students with severe disabilities?

A) Standardized end-of-year exams

B) Curriculum-Based Measurement (CBM)

C) High-stakes state testing

D) Intelligence quotient (IQ) tests

Assessing Students with Severe to Profound Disabilities

110. When assessing a nonverbal student's comprehension skills, which method would be most appropriate?

A) Administering a written multiple-choice test

B) Observing responses to visual or tactile prompts

C) Only asking verbal questions

D) Measuring verbal fluency

Data Collection and Progress Monitoring

111. What is the primary benefit of using data collection tools such as frequency charts and ABC (Antecedent-Behavior-Consequence) data?

A) To create long-term discipline records

B) To identify patterns in student behavior and adjust interventions

C) To replace the need for direct instruction

D) To document academic performance only

Legal and Ethical Considerations in Assessment

112. What legal requirement must be followed when selecting an assessment for a student with disabilities?

A) The test must be in the student's primary language and communication mode.

B) The student must take the test without accommodations.

C) The student must complete the same assessment as their general education peers.

D) Assessments should only focus on academic performance.

Section 4: Ethical and Legal Practice, Professionalism, and Collaboration

Special Education Laws and Regulations

113. Under IDEA, what is the primary purpose of transition planning in an IEP?

A) To prepare students for post-secondary education, employment, and independent living
B) To extend a student's school enrollment indefinitely
C) To eliminate the need for special education services
D) To restrict the student to a single career path

Ethical Responsibilities in Special Education

114. A teacher notices that a student's IEP goals have not been updated for two years. What is the teacher's ethical responsibility?

A) Ignore the issue unless the parents ask for changes
B) Inform the IEP team and schedule a review meeting
C) Make changes to the IEP without consulting the team
D) Reduce the student's instructional time

Collaboration with Stakeholders

115. What is the most effective way for special education teachers to support general education teachers in an inclusive classroom?

A) Co-teaching and providing resources tailored to student needs
B) Allowing general education teachers to handle all modifications alone

C) Removing students with disabilities from the classroom when challenges arise

D) Limiting collaboration to quarterly meetings

Advocacy and Professional Development

116. What is one of the best ways for a special education teacher to stay updated on new research and best practices?

A) Attending professional development workshops and special education conferences

B) Only relying on past experiences without updating strategies

C) Avoiding new research due to time constraints

D) Using outdated teaching methods for consistency

Section 1: Human Development and Individualized Learning Differences

Theories of Human Development

117. Which of the following best describes Vygotsky's concept of the Zone of Proximal Development (ZPD) in relation to students with disabilities?

A) Learning is best when tasks are slightly beyond a student's current ability, with support.

B) Students learn best when given complete independence in all activities.

C) A child's development is determined solely by innate abilities.

D) Social interaction has little effect on a student's cognitive growth.

Understanding Intellectual and Developmental Disabilities (IDD)

118. What is one of the most common co-occurring conditions in students with intellectual disabilities?

A) Attention Deficit Hyperactivity Disorder (ADHD)

B) Perfect motor coordination

C) Exceptional mathematical ability

D) Unusually fast language processing

Impact of Disabilities on Learning

119. A student with a profound disability has difficulty generalizing skills learned in therapy to the classroom. What is the best strategy to support skill transfer?

A) Providing instruction in multiple settings and contexts

B) Limiting instruction to one learning environment

C) Changing instructional methods frequently without consistency

D) Encouraging the student to figure it out independently

Individualized Learning Needs

120. What is the primary purpose of Universal Design for Learning (UDL) in special education?

A) To make learning accessible to all students through multiple means of engagement, representation, and action

B) To create the same instructional plan for every student

C) To eliminate the need for individualized supports

D) To restrict learning materials to text-based instruction only

Section 2: Planning and Instruction and the Learning Environment

Developing Individualized Education Programs (IEPs)

121. What is a key requirement of IEP goals?

A) Goals must be vague to allow for flexibility.

B) Goals should be specific, measurable, achievable, relevant, and time-bound (SMART).

C) Goals should be set only by teachers without parent input.

D) Goals should remain the same throughout the student's educational career.

Instructional Strategies for Severe to Profound Disabilities

122. Which instructional method is best suited for teaching daily living skills to students with severe disabilities?

A) Lecturing about daily routines

B) Direct, hands-on instruction with step-by-step modeling

C) Assigning reading materials on independent living

D) Providing a written test on self-care

Classroom and Environmental Modifications

123. What is the most effective environmental modification for a student with sensory processing disorder?

A) Keeping a structured, low-stimulation classroom with access to sensory tools

B) Using bright, flashing lights and unpredictable noises

C) Changing classroom routines daily without warning

D) Keeping the classroom loud and unstructured

Behavioral Interventions and Classroom Management

124. When implementing Positive Behavioral Interventions and Supports (PBIS), what is the primary goal?

A) To reinforce positive behaviors while minimizing challenging behaviors

B) To punish students for non-compliance

C) To remove students with disabilities from the general classroom

D) To ignore behaviors that interfere with learning

Section 3: Assessment

Types of Assessments in Special Education

125. What type of assessment is best suited for identifying a student's strengths and needs in a real-life setting?

A) Functional assessment

B) Standardized multiple-choice test

C) Timed IQ test

D) High-stakes state assessment

Assessing Students with Severe to Profound Disabilities

126. Which approach is best for assessing a student with a severe disability who has limited verbal communication?

A) Using a traditional written test

B) Observing the student in different settings and using alternative communication methods

C) Giving the same test as their peers without modifications

D) Relying only on teacher judgment without data collection

Data Collection and Progress Monitoring

127. What is the primary reason for using progress monitoring in special education?

A) To collect data to punish students for not meeting goals

B) To measure student growth and adjust instruction accordingly

C) To document failure rates for administrative records

D) To compare students with disabilities to their general education peers

Legal and Ethical Considerations in Assessment

128. Under IDEA, which factor must be considered when assessing students with disabilities?

A) Assessments must be administered in the student's preferred communication mode

B) Students must take the same test as their general education peers without modifications

C) No accommodations should be provided

D) Only one type of test should be used for decision-making

Section 4: Ethical and Legal Practice, Professionalism, and Collaboration

Special Education Laws and Regulations

129. Which of the following laws ensures that students with disabilities receive a Free Appropriate Public Education (FAPE)?

A) Individuals with Disabilities Education Act (IDEA)

B) No Child Left Behind Act (NCLB)

C) Every Student Succeeds Act (ESSA)

D) Family Educational Rights and Privacy Act (FERPA)

Ethical Responsibilities in Special Education

130. A special education teacher notices that a student's accommodations are not being implemented in the general education classroom. What should the teacher do?

A) Report the concern to the IEP team and collaborate with staff to ensure compliance

B) Ignore the issue and assume the student will adapt

C) Remove the student from the classroom

D) Change the accommodations without consulting the IEP team

Collaboration with Stakeholders

131. What is the most effective way to encourage parent involvement in the IEP process?

A) Scheduling regular meetings and maintaining open communication

B) Only informing parents about changes after they happen

C) Limiting parental input to academic subjects only

D) Avoiding parental involvement to reduce conflicts

Advocacy and Professional Development

132. What is one of the most effective ways for a special education teacher to advocate for students with severe disabilities?

A) Attending professional development sessions on best practices and special education law

B) Avoiding conversations about student needs with administrators

C) Limiting collaboration with colleagues

D) Using only outdated teaching methods

Section 1: Human Development and Individualized Learning Differences

Theories of Human Development

133. According to Bandura's Social Learning Theory, which factor plays a crucial role in the learning process?

A) Genetic predisposition only

B) Observation, modeling, and imitation

C) Memorization without interaction

D) Exclusive reliance on teacher-led instruction

Understanding Intellectual and Developmental Disabilities (IDD)

134. Which of the following is a defining characteristic of fetal alcohol spectrum disorder (FASD)?

A) Advanced verbal skills and rapid cognitive processing

B) Difficulty with impulse control, memory, and executive functioning

C) Significantly above-average IQ

D) Strong motor coordination and balance

Impact of Disabilities on Learning

135. Which of the following is a major challenge for students with profound disabilities in a classroom setting?

A) Mastering abstract mathematical concepts quickly

B) Generalizing skills learned in one context to another

C) Independent problem-solving with no guidance

D) Rapidly processing verbal instructions

Individualized Learning Needs

136. A teacher is working with a student who struggles with self-regulation. Which intervention would be most effective?

A) Providing a structured routine with clear expectations and visual supports

B) Allowing the student to self-monitor without guidance

C) Changing classroom rules frequently to encourage flexibility

D) Giving consequences without teaching replacement behaviors

Section 2: Planning and Instruction and the Learning Environment

Developing Individualized Education Programs (IEPs)

137. What is the purpose of the transition plan in an IEP?

A) To provide academic goals only

B) To prepare students for post-secondary education, employment, and independent living

C) To ensure students take the same curriculum as general education peers

D) To eliminate the need for support services after high school

Instructional Strategies for Severe to Profound Disabilities

138. Which teaching method is most effective for students with severe disabilities who require intensive support?

A) Lecture-based instruction with minimal engagement

B) Task analysis with step-by-step instruction and reinforcement

C) Independent learning with no intervention

D) Standardized textbook-based lessons

Classroom and Environmental Modifications

139. What is a key feature of a sensory-friendly classroom for students with severe disabilities?

A) Loud, unpredictable sounds to encourage alertness

B) A structured, low-stimulation environment with sensory tools

C) Frequent, unannounced changes in routine

D) Bright fluorescent lighting with no adjustments

Behavioral Interventions and Classroom Management

140. A student with a profound intellectual disability engages in repetitive rocking. What is the best approach for addressing this behavior?

A) Punishing the student for the behavior

B) Identifying the function of the behavior and providing appropriate sensory input

C) Removing the student from the classroom permanently

D) Ignoring the behavior completely

Section 3: Assessment

Types of Assessments in Special Education

141. Which type of assessment is best suited for measuring a student's ability to complete functional daily living skills?

A) Multiple-choice test

B) Functional skills checklist and observational assessment

C) Standardized math and reading exam

D) Timed academic proficiency test

Assessing Students with Severe to Profound Disabilities

142. A teacher wants to assess the communication skills of a nonverbal student. What method would be most appropriate?

A) Giving the student a written test

B) Observing their use of alternative communication methods (e.g., AAC devices, gestures, picture symbols)

C) Asking the student to read aloud

D) Assigning a verbal presentation

Data Collection and Progress Monitoring

143. Which data collection method is most effective for tracking a student's progress on a behavioral goal?

A) Randomized observations

B) Frequency recording, interval recording, and anecdotal notes

C) Relying on memory without documentation

D) Only reviewing progress once a year

Legal and Ethical Considerations in Assessment

144. Under the Individuals with Disabilities Education Act (IDEA), which requirement must be met when administering assessments to students with disabilities?

A) Assessments must be fair, nondiscriminatory, and administered in the student's primary language or mode of communication.

B) All students must take the same standardized test without modifications.

C) No accommodations are allowed.

D) Only teachers can decide which students need accommodations.

Section 4: Ethical and Legal Practice, Professionalism, and Collaboration

Special Education Laws and Regulations

145. What does the Least Restrictive Environment (LRE) principle require schools to do?

A) Educate students with disabilities in the most inclusive setting appropriate to their needs

B) Place all students with disabilities in separate classrooms

C) Require all students to receive identical instruction

D) Prohibit students with disabilities from receiving additional support

Ethical Responsibilities in Special Education

146. A teacher discovers that a student with disabilities is not receiving the accommodations outlined in their IEP. What is the teacher's ethical obligation?

A) Document the issue and report it to the appropriate school personnel to ensure compliance

B) Ignore the issue to avoid confrontation

C) Remove the student from general education classes

D) Modify the accommodations without consulting the IEP team

Collaboration with Stakeholders

147. Which strategy is most effective in building a strong collaborative relationship between special education teachers and parents?

A) Regular, open communication and involving parents in decision-making

B) Only discussing student progress at annual IEP meetings

C) Avoiding parent input to maintain authority in decision-making

D) Limiting communication to emails only

Advocacy and Professional Development

148. What is one of the best ways for special education teachers to stay informed about best practices?

A) Attending professional development workshops, conferences, and training sessions

B) Relying only on past experiences without updating strategies

C) Avoiding collaboration with other educators

D) Using outdated teaching methods for consistency

Section 1: Human Development and Individualized Learning Differences

Theories of Human Development

149. According to Piaget's cognitive development theory, which stage is characterized by the development of logical thought but difficulty with abstract concepts?

A) Sensorimotor

B) Preoperational

C) Concrete Operational

D) Formal Operational

Understanding Intellectual and Developmental Disabilities (IDD)

150. Which of the following is a key characteristic of students with Rett Syndrome?

A) Progressive loss of motor skills and repetitive hand movements

B) High levels of social interaction and communication skills

C) Increased muscle strength over time

D) Strong independent living skills

Impact of Disabilities on Learning

151. A student with severe disabilities has difficulty interpreting social cues. Which condition is most likely to be associated with this challenge?

A) Attention Deficit Hyperactivity Disorder (ADHD)

B) Autism Spectrum Disorder (ASD)

C) Dyscalculia

D) Visual impairment

Individualized Learning Needs

152. Which of the following is the best instructional approach for a student with profound intellectual disabilities who has a very short attention span?

A) Long lecture-based lessons

B) Short, repetitive tasks with immediate reinforcement

C) Independent study without teacher interaction

D) Standardized testing as the primary instructional tool

Section 2: Planning and Instruction and the Learning Environment

Developing Individualized Education Programs (IEPs)

153. Which component must be included in an IEP according to federal law?

A) The student's favorite activities

B) Measurable annual goals that address the student's needs

C) A list of all possible accommodations for every student

D) The same educational objectives as their grade-level peers

Instructional Strategies for Severe to Profound Disabilities

154. What is the most effective way to teach self-care skills to students with severe disabilities?

A) Provide step-by-step direct instruction with real-life practice

B) Expect students to observe and imitate without direct instruction

C) Use written explanations without hands-on practice

D) Focus only on academic subjects and avoid self-care training

Classroom and Environmental Modifications

155. What is an example of an effective environmental modification for a student with visual impairments?

A) Keeping all classroom materials in random locations

B) Using high-contrast materials and tactile labels

C) Minimizing classroom organization to encourage independence

D) Using only auditory instruction without visual support

Behavioral Interventions and Classroom Management

156. A teacher implements a behavior intervention plan (BIP) for a student with frequent aggression. What is the primary purpose of this plan?

A) To provide positive strategies that replace aggressive behaviors

B) To punish the student when aggression occurs

C) To remove the student from the classroom

D) To eliminate all interactions with peers

Section 3: Assessment

Types of Assessments in Special Education

157. Which assessment type is best suited for measuring a student's progress toward individualized functional goals?

A) Standardized academic testing

B) Curriculum-Based Measurement (CBM)

C) High-stakes state testing

D) Verbal intelligence testing

Assessing Students with Severe to Profound Disabilities

158. A teacher wants to evaluate a nonverbal student's ability to recognize basic symbols for communication. Which method would be most appropriate?

A) Administering a written exam

B) Observing the student's response to visual communication boards

C) Asking the student to verbalize their answers

D) Requiring the student to complete a reading comprehension test

Data Collection and Progress Monitoring

159. What is the best way to monitor a student's progress on a self-care goal, such as brushing their teeth?

A) Recording the frequency of successful attempts over time

B) Relying on verbal reports from the student

C) Giving a written quiz about hygiene

D) Only checking progress once per year

Legal and Ethical Considerations in Assessment

160. When conducting assessments, what is the primary legal requirement under IDEA?

A) Assessments must be tailored to the student's individual communication and learning needs.

B) All students must take the same assessment without modifications.

C) No accommodations should be provided.

D) Testing should focus only on academic subjects.

Section 4: Ethical and Legal Practice, Professionalism, and Collaboration

Special Education Laws and Regulations

161. Under the Americans with Disabilities Act (AD A), what is a school's responsibility toward students with disabilities?

A) Providing equal access and reasonable accommodations in school programs

B) Placing all students with disabilities in separate classrooms

C) Limiting access to specialized services

D) Eliminating special education services

Ethical Responsibilities in Special Education

162. If a teacher suspects a student with an IEP is not receiving required accommodations, what should they do?

A) Document concerns and collaborate with the IEP team to ensure compliance

B) Ignore the issue unless the parent complains

C) Remove the student from general education classes

D) Change the accommodations without consulting the IEP team

Collaboration with Stakeholders

163. What is the best strategy for fostering collaboration between special education and general education teachers?

A) Regular co-planning meetings and shared instructional strategies

B) Limiting communication to emergencies only

C) Keeping special education students entirely separate from general education peers

D) Avoiding collaboration to minimize workload

Advocacy and Professional Development

164. What is one way special education teachers can advocate for students with severe disabilities?

A) Participating in policy discussions and professional development opportunities

B) Avoiding communication with administrators about student needs

C) Limiting participation in IEP meetings

D) Using outdated instructional methods

Section 1: Human Development and Individualized Learning Differences

Theories of Human Development

165. Which of the following best represents Bronfenbrenner's ecological systems theory in relation to students with disabilities?

A) Development is solely determined by genetic factors.
B) A child's development is influenced by multiple environmental systems, including family, school, and society.
C) Peer interactions have no effect on development.
D) The physical classroom environment has no impact on learning.

Understanding Intellectual and Developmental Disabilities (IDD)

166. Which condition is most commonly associated with difficulties in verbal communication and social interactions?

A) Autism Spectrum Disorder (ASD)
B) Muscular Dystrophy
C) Dyslexia
D) Cerebral Palsy (without intellectual impairment)

Impact of Disabilities on Learning

167. A student with an intellectual disability struggles with memory retention. Which instructional strategy would be most effective?

A) Teaching large amounts of information at once
B) Using repetition, chunking, and visual supports
C) Limiting the use of visual aids
D) Expecting the student to memorize content independently

Individualized Learning Needs

168. What is the primary benefit of using assistive technology for students with severe disabilities?

A) It replaces the need for a special education teacher.

B) It provides alternative ways for students to communicate, learn, and partici-pate.

C) It eliminates the need for individualized instruction.

D) It ensures that all students can complete the same assignments as their peers.

Section 2: Planning and Instruction and the Learning Environment

Developing Individualized Education Programs (IEPs)

169. Which of the following is a legally required component of an IEP?

A) The student's favorite classroom activities

B) A detailed lesson plan for every school day

C) Present levels of academic and functional performance

D) The same curriculum as all general education students

Instructional Strategies for Severe to Profound Disabilities

170. What is the most effective way to teach vocational skills to students with severe disabilities?

A) Lecture-based learning with written assignments

B) Hands-on training with real-world practice and job coaching

C) Only theoretical discussions without practical application

D) Relying on standardized tests to measure job readiness

Classroom and Environmental Modifications

171. Which classroom adaptation would best support a student with sensory processing disorder?

A) Bright, flashing lights and unpredictable noises

B) A quiet area with dim lighting and sensory-friendly seating

C) Changing the classroom layout daily

D) Exposing the student to constant auditory and visual stimuli

Behavioral Interventions and Classroom Management

172. A student frequently engages in self-injurious behavior. What is the most appropriate first step for the teacher?

A) Implementing a Functional Behavior Assessment (FB A) to determine the behavior's function

B) Ignoring the behavior and hoping it stops

C) Restricting the student's movement

D) Removing all reinforcers

Section 3: Assessment

Types of Assessments in Special Education

173. What type of assessment is most appropriate for tracking a student's ability to complete multi-step tasks over time?

A) Standardized achievement test

B) Portfolio assessment

C) Single timed evaluation

D) High-stakes exit exam

Assessing Students with Severe to Profound Disabilities

174. A teacher needs to assess a nonverbal student's understanding of basic concepts. Which method would be most effective?

A) Traditional paper-and-pencil test

B) Observing the student's use of visual supports and AAC devices

C) Requiring the student to verbally respond to questions

D) Administering a standardized reading comprehension test

Data Collection and Progress Monitoring

175. What is the most effective way to collect behavioral data for a student who exhibits self-stimulatory behavior?

A) Use an ABC (Antecedent-Behavior-Consequence) chart to track patterns.

B) Only rely on occasional teacher recollections.

C) Remove the student from class when behaviors occur.

D) Ignore the behaviors unless they escalate.

Legal and Ethical Considerations in Assessment

176. When assessing students with disabilities, which legal requirement must be followed?

A) Assessments must be adapted to the student's communication and learning needs.

B) All students must take assessments in the same format.

C) No modifications are allowed for any student.

D) Assessment accommodations must be identical for all students.

Section 4: Ethical and Legal Practice, Professionalism, and Collaboration

Special Education Laws and Regulations

177. Under the Free Appropriate Public Education (FAPE) mandate, what are schools required to provide for students with disabilities?

A) Specialized instruction and related services at no cost to parents

B) Education only in segregated settings

C) Exemptions from all assessments

D) No services beyond what is offered to general education students

Ethical Responsibilities in Special Education

178. A teacher suspects that a student's disability is not being properly accommodated. What should they do first?

A) Communicate concerns with the IEP team and advocate for appropriate services.

B) Ignore the situation unless a parent complains.

C) Unilaterally change the accommodations without consulting the team.

D) Remove the student from the general education classroom.

Collaboration with Stakeholders

179. What is one of the most effective ways for teachers to collaborate with parents of students with disabilities?

A) Holding regular meetings and providing updates on progress

B) Only contacting parents when a problem arises

C) Limiting parental involvement in decision-making

D) Avoiding discussions about student challenges

Advocacy and Professional Development

180. How can special education teachers stay updated on best practices in the field?

A) Attending professional development workshops and conferences

B) Relying solely on personal teaching experience

C) Avoiding collaboration with colleagues

D) Using outdated materials and instructional methods

Section 1: Human Development and Individualized Learning Differences

Theories of Human Development

181. According to Erikson's stages of psychosocial development, which stage is most relevant for school-aged children developing a sense of competence?

A) Trust vs. Mistrust

B) Initiative vs. Guilt

C) Industry vs. Inferiority

D) Identity vs. Role Confusion

Understanding Intellectual and Developmental Disabilities (IDD)

182. Which of the following is a common characteristic of Fragile X Syndrome?

A) High muscle tone and overdeveloped speech skills

B) Social anxiety, speech delays, and repetitive behaviors

C) Rapid acquisition of academic skills without intervention

D) Severe vision impairment as the primary disability

Impact of Disabilities on Learning

183. A student with cerebral palsy has difficulty with fine motor control. Which classroom activity might be most challenging for them?

A) Listening to a lecture

B) Writing with a pencil for an extended period

C) Participating in group discussions

D) Watching a video lesson

Individualized Learning Needs

184. Which instructional strategy is most beneficial for students with severe intellectual disabilities?

A) Passive listening to long lectures

B) Hands-on, multi-sensory activities with repetition

C) Sole reliance on standardized textbooks

D) Independent study with minimal support

Section 2: Planning and Instruction and the Learning Environment

Developing Individualized Education Programs (IEPs)

185. What is the primary goal of an IEP for a student with severe disabilities?

A) To provide a general education curriculum without modifications

B) To address the student's unique needs through individualized goals and supports

C) To follow the same instructional methods for all students

D) To focus only on academic skills and not life skills

Instructional Strategies for Severe to Profound Disabilities

186. What is the most effective approach for teaching a student with a profound disability to use an adaptive communication device?

A) Providing the device without instruction

B) Modeling its use consistently and reinforcing correct attempts

C) Expecting the student to explore the device independently

D) Using the device only for testing situations

Classroom and Environmental Modifications

187. A teacher wants to create an inclusive classroom for students with sensory sensitivities. Which strategy would be most beneficial?

A) Keeping the classroom bright and noisy to promote alertness

B) Providing a quiet area with dim lighting and noise-reducing headphones

C) Constantly changing the classroom layout to prevent predictability

D) Avoiding sensory accommodations to encourage adaptation

Behavioral Interventions and Classroom Management

188. What is the most effective way to decrease self-injurious behaviors in a student with severe disabilities?

A) Implementing a Functional Behavior Assessment (FB A) to determine the cause

B) Ignoring the behavior entirely

C) Using punishment as the primary intervention

D) Restricting the student's access to all classroom activities

Section 3: Assessment

Types of Assessments in Special Education

189. Which type of assessment is most useful for measuring a student's progress toward mastering a life skill such as dressing independently?

A) Multiple-choice written exam

B) Curriculum-Based Measurement (CBM)

C) Functional skills checklist and observational assessment

D) Standardized intelligence test

Assessing Students with Severe to Profound Disabilities

190. A nonverbal student is being assessed for their ability to recognize colors. What would be the most appropriate method?

A) Asking the student to verbally name colors

B) Having the student match colored cards or use an AAC device

C) Giving the student a written test on colors

D) Using a high-stakes standardized test

Data Collection and Progress Monitoring

191. A teacher wants to measure how often a student engages in self-stimulatory behaviors. What is the best method?

A) Frequency recording and interval recording

B) Guessing the approximate frequency based on past observations

C) Giving a verbal questionnaire to the student

D) Relying on annual standardized test scores

Legal and Ethical Considerations in Assessment

192. Under IDEA, which requirement must be met when assessing students with disabilities?

A) The assessment must be conducted in the student's primary language or mode of communication.

B) The student must take the same assessment as their general education peers without modifications.

C) Testing accommodations should never be provided.

D) Standardized tests should be the only method of assessment used.

Section 4: Ethical and Legal Practice, Professionalism, and Collaboration

Special Education Laws and Regulations

193. The Least Restrictive Environment (LRE) principle in IDEA requires that students with disabilities be educated:

A) In a separate classroom away from their peers

B) In the most inclusive setting appropriate for their needs

C) Only with other students who have the same disability

D) Exclusively at home with limited school interaction

Ethical Responsibilities in Special Education

194. A teacher observes that a student with a disability is not receiving their mandated IEP accommodations. What should the teacher do?

A) Report the concern to the IEP team and work on a resolution

B) Ignore the issue since it is not their responsibility

C) Remove the student from the general education classroom

D) Change the IEP accommodations without notifying the team

Collaboration with Stakeholders

195. What is the most effective way for special education teachers to collaborate with general education teachers?

A) Providing training on instructional strategies for students with disabilities

B) Keeping special education students separate from general education classes

C) Limiting communication to email only

D) Letting general education teachers manage all special education modifications independently

Advocacy and Professional Development

196. How can special education teachers stay informed about the latest research and best practices in the field?

A) Attending professional development workshops and special education conferences

B) Relying solely on past experience without updating strategies

C) Avoiding discussions with other educators about new methods

D) Using outdated instructional materials

Section 1: Human Development and Individualized Learning Differences

Theories of Human Development

197. Which of the following best represents the concept of scaffolding in Vygotsky's theory of development?

A) Encouraging students to learn completely independently

B) Providing step-by-step support that is gradually reduced as the student gains independence

C) Limiting learning opportunities to only teacher-directed instruction

D) Relying solely on peer-to-peer instruction without adult intervention

Understanding Intellectual and Developmental Disabilities (IDD)

198. Which of the following is a primary characteristic of Down Syndrome?

A) Progressive loss of vision and hearing

B) Distinct facial features, intellectual disability, and delayed speech development

C) A complete lack of communication ability

D) Rapid acquisition of complex academic skills

Impact of Disabilities on Learning

199. How does a learning disability primarily affect a student?

A) It impairs overall intelligence.

B) It interferes with specific academic skills such as reading, writing, or math.

C) It prevents students from attending school.

D) It only affects motor skills.

Individualized Learning Needs

200. A student with a severe disability is struggling to follow multi-step directions. What is the best strategy to support their comprehension?

A) Provide one-step instructions with visual and verbal cues.

B) Give all steps at once and expect the student to follow independently.

C) Avoid using instructional supports.

D) Require the student to figure out the task without assistance.

6.2 ANSWER SHEET – PRACTICE TEST 2

101. Answer: B) Autonomy vs. Shame and Doubt

Explanation: During the Autonomy vs. Shame and Doubt stage (ages 1-3), children develop a sense of independence. For children with disabilities, fostering autonomy through structured choices and self-help skills is crucial.

102. Answer: A) Excessive appetite and food-seeking behavior

Explanation: Prader-Willi Syndrome is a genetic disorder that often leads to constant hunger, intellectual disabilities, and behavioral challenges. Careful meal planning and behavioral support are essential.

103. Answer: B) Providing written and visual instructions along with verbal cues

Explanation: Students with processing difficulties benefit from multi-modal instruction, which includes auditory, visual, and kinesthetic supports to reinforce learning.

104. Answer: B) The student's individualized learning style and needs

Explanation: Instruction should be tailored to a student's individual strengths, abilities, and needs rather than following a one-size-fits-all approach.

105. Answer: C) Measurable annual goals based on the student's present levels of performance

Explanation: An IEP must include specific, measurable goals that address academic and functional skills, ensuring accountability and progress monitoring.

106. Answer: B) Encouraging the use of Augmentative and Alternative Communication (AAC) devices

Explanation: AAC tools, such as picture exchange communication systems (PECS) or speech-generating devices, help nonverbal students effectively communicate and participate in learning.

107. Answer: B) A structured, predictable environment with accessible materials

Explanation: A structured classroom helps students with disabilities feel secure and promotes engagement through clear routines, visual supports, and accessible materials.

108. Answer: B) Providing alternative behaviors that fulfill the same function

Explanation: Replacing self-injurious behaviors with functionally equivalent, safe alternatives (e.g., sensory tools, communication devices) helps students meet their needs in a healthier way.

109. Answer: B) Curriculum-Based Measurement (CBM)

Explanation: CBMs track student progress in small, measurable steps, making them ideal for students with severe disabilities who require frequent monitoring and individualized instruction.

110. Answer: B) Observing responses to visual or tactile prompts

Explanation: Nonverbal students can demonstrate comprehension through alternative means, such as pointing to pictures, using AAC devices, or responding to hands-on materials.

111. Answer: B) To identify patterns in student behavior and adjust interventions

Explanation: Tracking behavior helps educators understand triggers, develop proactive interventions, and measure the effectiveness of behavior support plans.

112. Answer: A) The test must be in the student's primary language and communication mode.

Explanation: Under IDEA, assessments must be accessible, meaning they should be conducted in a way that accurately measures the student's abilities, including through assistive technology or alternative communication methods.

113. Answer: A) To prepare students for post-secondary education, employment, and independent living

Explanation: Transition planning, required by IDEA at age 16 (or earlier in some states), helps students with disabilities prepare for life after high school by setting realistic goals for employment, education, and independent living.

114. Answer: B) Inform the IEP team and schedule a review meeting

Explanation: IEPs must be reviewed at least annually to ensure goals are current and appropriate. Teachers must advocate for regular updates when needed.

115. Answer: A) Co-teaching and providing resources tailored to student needs

Explanation: Collaboration through co-teaching, shared planning, and providing differentiated materials ensures that students with disabilities receive appropriate support in inclusive settings.

116. Answer: A) Attending professional development workshops and special education conferences

Explanation: Ongoing professional development helps teachers stay informed about new instructional strategies, legal updates, and evidence-based interventions for students with disabilities.

117. Answer: A) Learning is best when tasks are slightly beyond a student's current ability, with support.

Explanation: The Zone of Proximal Development (ZPD) suggests that students learn best when working on tasks that are just beyond their independent ability, with the support of teachers, peers, or caregivers.

118. Answer: A) Attention Deficit Hyperactivity Disorder (ADHD)

Explanation: Many students with intellectual disabilities also experience ADHD, which can affect focus, impulse control, and task completion.

119. Answer: A) Providing instruction in multiple settings and contexts

Explanation: Students with profound disabilities often struggle to generalize skills across different environments. Teaching the skill in multiple settings helps reinforce learning.

120. Answer: A) To make learning accessible to all students through multiple means of engagement, representation, and action

Explanation: UDL is an instructional framework that provides diverse ways for students to access content, express learning, and stay engaged, ensuring accessibility for all learners.

121. Answer: B) Goals should be specific, measurable, achievable, relevant, and time-bound (SMART).

Explanation: SMART goals ensure that student progress is clearly defined and can be accurately measured.

122. Answer: B) Direct, hands-on instruction with step-by-step modeling

Explanation: Students with severe disabilities benefit from hands-on learning experiences that model functional skills in real-life contexts.

123. Answer: A) Keeping a structured, low-stimulation classroom with access to sensory tools

Explanation: A structured, predictable classroom with sensory-friendly supports helps students with sensory processing difficulties stay regulated and engaged.

124. Answer: A) To reinforce positive behaviors while minimizing challenging behaviors

Explanation: PBIS is a proactive approach that promotes positive behaviors through reinforcement, structured routines, and individualized supports.

125. Answer: A) Functional assessment

Explanation: Functional assessments evaluate a student's ability to perform everyday tasks, such as self-care, communication, and social interactions, making them essential for students with severe disabilities.

126. Answer: B) Observing the student in different settings and using alternative communication methods

Explanation: Observational assessments, along with AAC (Augmentative and Alternative Communication) tools, allow students with limited verbal skills to demonstrate understanding and abilities.

127. Answer: B) To measure student growth and adjust instruction accordingly

Explanation: Progress monitoring allows teachers to track a student's improvement over time and make necessary instructional modifications.

128. Answer: A) Assessments must be administered in the student's preferred communication mode

Explanation: IDEA ensures that students with disabilities receive fair assessments by allowing accommodations such as sign language interpreters, braille, or speech-to-text tools.

129. Answer: A) Individuals with Disabilities Education Act (IDEA)

Explanation: IDEA mandates that all students with disabilities receive a Free Appropriate Public Education (FAPE), including necessary supports and services.

130. Answer: A) Report the concern to the IEP team and collaborate with staff to ensure compliance

Explanation: Teachers must advocate for students and ensure that accommodations outlined in the IEP are implemented appropriately.

131. Answer: A) Scheduling regular meetings and maintaining open communication

Explanation: Frequent communication and collaboration with parents help ensure that students receive consistent support across school and home environments.

132. Answer: A) Attending professional development sessions on best practices and special education law

Explanation: Ongoing professional development ensures that teachers remain informed about new research, instructional strategies, and legal requirements for students with disabilities.

133. Answer: B) Observation, modeling, and imitation

Explanation: Bandura's Social Learning Theory states that people learn behaviors, attitudes, and skills by observing others. This is especially relevant for students with disabilities who may benefit from peer modeling and structured observation opportunities.

134. Answer: B) Difficulty with impulse control, memory, and executive functioning

Explanation: FASD affects cognitive function, behavior, and executive functioning, making learning and self-regulation difficult. Many students with FASD require consistent routines, visual supports, and explicit instruction.

135. Answer: B) Generalizing skills learned in one context to another

Explanation: Students with severe disabilities often struggle with applying learned skills across different settings. Teaching strategies should include structured repetition in multiple environments to reinforce learning.

136. Answer: A) Providing a structured routine with clear expectations and visual supports

Explanation: Students with self-regulation challenges benefit from consistent routines, clear expectations, and visual cues that help them navigate transitions and behavioral expectations.

137. Answer: B) To prepare students for post-secondary education, employment, and independent living

Explanation: Transition planning, required under IDEA, helps students develop skills necessary for success after high school. It includes **vocational training, life skills, and independent living supports.**

138. Answer: B) Task analysis with step-by-step instruction and reinforcement

Explanation: Task analysis breaks down complex skills into manageable steps, ensuring students receive repeated, structured instruction that reinforces learning.

139. Answer: B) A structured, low-stimulation environment with sensory tools

Explanation: Many students with sensory processing disorders benefit from a predictable, structured classroom with appropriate sensory supports (e.g., fidget tools, weighted blankets).

140. Answer: B) Identifying the function of the behavior and providing appropriate sensory input

Explanation: Repetitive behaviors (stimming) often serve sensory or self-regulation functions. Identifying the cause and providing **alternative sensory strategies** can help manage behaviors effectively.

141. Answer: B) Functional skills checklist and observational assessment

Explanation: Functional assessments evaluate how well a student performs essential life tasks, such as dressing, preparing food, and communication, making them more relevant for students with severe disabilities.

142. **Answer:** B) Observing their use of alternative communication methods (e.g., AAC devices, gestures, picture symbols)

Explanation: Nonverbal students often communicate using Augmentative and Alternative Communication (AAC) methods, making observational assessments the most effective way to measure their communication abilities.

143. **Answer:** B) Frequency recording, interval recording, and anecdotal notes

Explanation: Systematic data collection ensures that teachers can accurately track behavior patterns and make informed decisions about interventions.

144. **Answer:** A) Assessments must be fair, nondiscriminatory, and administered in the student's primary language or mode of communication.

Explanation: IDEA requires that all assessments be adapted to ensure that students with disabilities can demonstrate their abilities accurately.

145. **Answer:** A) Educate students with disabilities in the most inclusive setting appropriate to their needs

Explanation: LRE ensures that students with disabilities receive education alongside their peers as much as possible while receiving necessary supports and accommodations.

146. **Answer:** A) Document the issue and report it to the appropriate school personnel to ensure compliance

Explanation: Educators have an ethical and legal responsibility to advocate for students and ensure that IEP accommodations are implemented as required.

147. Answer: A) Regular, open communication and involving parents in decision-making

Explanation: Parents are key partners in their child's education. Regular collaboration helps create consistent support across home and school environments.

148. Answer: A) Attending professional development workshops, conferences, and training sessions

Explanation: Continuous professional development helps teachers stay updated on research-based strategies, legal requirements, and instructional innovations in special education.

149. Answer: C) Concrete Operational

Explanation: The Concrete Operational stage (ages 7-11) is when children begin using logical thought processes but still struggle with abstract ideas. This understanding is essential when designing instructional strategies for students with severe disabilities.

150. Answer: A) Progressive loss of motor skills and repetitive hand movements

Explanation: Rett Syndrome is a genetic disorder primarily affecting females, leading to loss of motor skills, communication difficulties, and repetitive hand movements.

151. Answer: B) Autism Spectrum Disorder (ASD)

Explanation: Students with ASD often struggle with understanding social interactions, nonverbal communication, and peer relationships.

152. Answer: B) Short, repetitive tasks with immediate reinforcement

Explanation: Breaking tasks into small, manageable steps and using immediate reinforcement helps students with profound disabilities remain engaged and learn effectively.

153. Answer: B) Measurable annual goals that address the student's needs

Explanation: IDEA mandates that IEPs include measurable annual goals to track student progress in academic and functional areas.

154. Answer: A) Provide step-by-step direct instruction with real-life practice

Explanation: Explicit, hands-on instruction using task analysis helps students learn essential self-care skills.

155. Answer: B) Using high-contrast materials and tactile labels

Explanation: Providing high-contrast visuals and tactile markers helps students with visual impairments navigate the classroom and access learning materials.

156. Answer: A) To provide positive strategies that replace aggressive behaviors

Explanation: A BIP focuses on teaching alternative behaviors and reducing problem behaviors using reinforcement and structured interventions.

157. Answer: B) Curriculum-Based Measurement (CBM)

Explanation: CBM is used to track progress on individualized goals, making it an effective tool for assessing students with severe disabilities in functional and academic areas.

158. Answer: B) Observing the student's response to visual communication boards

Explanation: Observational assessments help measure communication abilities in nonverbal students who rely on alternative communication systems.

159. Answer: A) Recording the frequency of successful attempts over time

Explanation: Tracking the frequency of independent attempts helps teachers measure progress and adjust instruction as needed.

160. Answer: A) Assessments must be tailored to the student's individual communication and learning needs.

Explanation: IDEA requires assessments to be adapted based on the student's abilities to ensure accurate measurement of their strengths and needs.

161. Answer: A) Providing equal access and reasonable accommodations in school programs

Explanation: The ADA ensures that students with disabilities receive equal opportunities and necessary accommodations in education and public settings.

162. Answer: A) Document concerns and collaborate with the IEP team to ensure compliance

Explanation: Teachers have an ethical responsibility to ensure that students receive the support outlined in their IEPs.

163. Answer: A) Regular co-planning meetings and shared instructional strategies

Explanation: Co-planning and collaboration between teachers ensure that students receive consistent support and inclusive instruction.

164. Answer: A) Participating in policy discussions and professional development opportunities

Explanation: Advocacy includes staying informed on best practices, engaging in educational policy, and ensuring students receive appropriate services.

165. Answer: B) A child's development is influenced by multiple environmental systems, including family, school, and society.

Explanation: Bronfenbrenner's theory emphasizes how different environments (microsystem, mesosystem, exosystem, and macrosystem) interact to shape a child's development.

166. Answer: A) Autism Spectrum Disorder (ASD)

Explanation: ASD is characterized by challenges in social communication, repetitive behaviors, and difficulty with verbal and nonverbal communication.

167. Answer: B) Using repetition, chunking, and visual supports

Explanation: Breaking information into smaller chunks, reinforcing learning through repetition, and providing visual cues help students with memory difficulties.

168. Answer: B) It provides alternative ways for students to communicate, learn, and participate.

Explanation: Assistive technology, such as speech-generating devices, adaptive keyboards, and communication apps, helps students with disabilities engage in learning and communication.

169. **Answer:** C) Present levels of academic and functional performance

Explanation: An IEP must include a description of the student's current abilities and needs to establish appropriate goals and services.

170. **Answer:** B) Hands-on training with real-world practice and job coaching

Explanation: Vocational training should include direct, hands-on experience, task analysis, and job coaching to build independence.

171. **Answer:** B) A quiet area with dim lighting and sensory-friendly seating

Explanation: Providing a sensory-friendly environment helps students with sensory processing challenges self-regulate and focus on learning.

172. **Answer:** A) Implementing a Functional Behavior Assessment (FB A) to determine the behavior's function

Explanation: An FBA identifies the causes of challenging behaviors, allowing for targeted interventions and positive reinforcement strategies.

173. **Answer:** B) Portfolio assessment

Explanation: Portfolio assessments compile work samples, observations, and progress over time, making them ideal for tracking multi-step skill development in students with disabilities.

174. **Answer:** B) Observing the student's use of visual supports and AAC devices

Explanation: Nonverbal students often rely on alternative communication systems (e.g., PECS, AAC devices), making observation the best assessment method.

175. **Answer:** A) Use an ABC (Antecedent-Behavior-Consequence) chart to track patterns.

Explanation: ABC data collection helps identify triggers (antecedents), behaviors, and consequences, allowing educators to develop appropriate interventions.

176. **Answer:** A) Assessments must be adapted to the student's communication and learning needs.

Explanation: IDEA mandates that assessments must be nondiscriminatory and accessible for students with disabilities.

177. **Answer:** A) Specialized instruction and related services at no cost to parents

Explanation: FAPE guarantees that students with disabilities receive appropriate educational services without financial burden on families.

178. **Answer:** A) Communicate concerns with the IEP team and advocate for appropriate services.

Explanation: Teachers have an ethical obligation to ensure that students receive the support outlined in their IEPs.

179. **Answer:** A) Holding regular meetings and providing updates on progress

Explanation: Regular communication with parents builds strong partnerships that support student success.

180. Answer: A) Attending professional development workshops and conferences

Explanation: Ongoing professional development ensures that teachers remain informed about new strategies, research, and legal requirements in special education.

181. Answer: C) Industry vs. Inferiority

Explanation: Children in the industry vs. inferiority stage (ages 6-12) develop a sense of competence through learning and completing tasks. Encouraging success in school settings helps build confidence.

182. Answer: B) Social anxiety, speech delays, and repetitive behaviors

Explanation: Fragile X Syndrome is a genetic condition that often results in social anxiety, speech delays, repetitive behaviors, and cognitive impairments.

183. Answer: B) Writing with a pencil for an extended period

Explanation: Cerebral palsy can affect muscle control and coordination, making fine motor tasks like handwriting difficult. Alternative tools such as speech-to-text or adaptive keyboards can help.

184. Answer: B) Hands-on, multi-sensory activities with repetition

Explanation: Students with severe disabilities benefit from structured, repetitive, and multi-sensory learning experiences that reinforce concepts in a meaningful way.

185. Answer: B) To address the student's unique needs through individualized goals and supports

Explanation: An IEP is designed to provide customized educational goals, accommodations, and services to meet a student's unique learning needs.

186. Answer: B) Modeling its use consistently and reinforcing correct attempts

Explanation: Students need consistent modeling, guided practice, and reinforcement to become proficient in using adaptive communication tools.

187. Answer: B) Providing a quiet area with dim lighting and noise-reducing headphones

Explanation: Creating a sensory-friendly environment with calming spaces helps students with sensory sensitivities self-regulate and focus on learning.

188. Answer: A) Implementing a Functional Behavior Assessment (FB A) to determine the cause

Explanation: An FBA helps identify the triggers of self-injurious behaviors, allowing educators to develop positive interventions and replacement behaviors.

189. Answer: C) Functional skills checklist and observational assessment

Explanation: Functional assessments track a student's ability to perform real-world skills, making them ideal for assessing progress in life skills such as dressing, eating, and self-care.

190. Answer: B) Having the student match colored cards or use an AAC device

Explanation: Students who are nonverbal can demonstrate understanding through matching tasks, pointing, or using assistive communication devices.

191. Answer: A) Frequency recording and interval recording

Explanation: Systematic data collection methods such as frequency recording (counting occurrences) and interval recording (tracking behaviors in set time periods) provide accurate behavioral data.

192. Answer: A) The assessment must be conducted in the student's primary language or mode of communication.

Explanation: IDEA requires that assessments be administered in a way that accurately measures the student's abilities, including through assistive technology or alternative formats.

193. Answer: B) In the most inclusive setting appropriate for their needs

Explanation: LRE ensures that students with disabilities learn alongside their peers as much as possible, with necessary supports and accommodations.

194. Answer: A) Report the concern to the IEP team and work on a resolution

Explanation: Educators have a legal and ethical obligation to ensure that students receive the accommodations specified in their IEPs.

195. Answer: A) Providing training on instructional strategies for students with disabilities

Explanation: Collaboration includes sharing strategies, co-teaching, and ensuring that all teachers understand best practices for supporting students with disabilities.

196. Answer: A) Attending professional development workshops and special education conferences

Explanation: Continuing education ensures that special education teachers stay current on research, instructional strategies, and legal updates.

197. Answer: B) Providing step-by-step support that is gradually reduced as the student gains independence

Explanation: Scaffolding is an instructional technique where teachers provide structured support as students develop new skills, gradually reducing assistance as mastery increases.

198. Answer: B) Distinct facial features, intellectual disability, and delayed speech development

Explanation: Down Syndrome is a genetic condition associated with characteristic facial features, mild to moderate intellectual disability, and delays in language development.

199. Answer: B) It interferes with specific academic skills such as reading, writing, or math.

Explanation: Learning disabilities do not impact overall intelligence but affect specific areas of learning, such as dyslexia (reading), dysgraphia (writing), and dyscalculia (math).

200. Answer: A) Provide one-step instructions with visual and verbal cues.

Explanation: Breaking down tasks into single steps and reinforcing them with visuals and verbal guidance helps students with severe disabilities process information more effectively.

TEST-TAKING STRATEGIES

Preparing for the **Praxis Special Education: Severe to Profound (5547) Exam** is only half the battle—**knowing how to take the test effectively** is equally important. This section provides **strategies to maximize performance** on test day and **techniques to overcome test anxiety** to ensure a confident, stress-free testing experience.

Test-Taking Strategies for the Praxis 5547 Exam

1. Understand the Exam Format

- The Praxis 5547 exam consists of **approximately 120 multiple-choice questions**.

- You have **2 hours (120 minutes)** to complete the test.

- Questions cover **four major sections**:
  Human Development and Individualized Learning Differences
  Planning and Instruction and the Learning Environment
  Assessment
  Ethical and Legal Practice, Professionalism, and Collaboration

Strategy: Familiarize yourself with the exam structure in advance to avoid surprises.

2. Manage Your Time Wisely

- You have **approximately 1 minute per question**.

- **Avoid spending too much time on any single question**—if you're unsure, mark it for review and move on.

- Budget your time as follows:

Section	Time Allocation
Human Development & Learning Differences	30 minutes
Planning & Instruction	35 minutes
Assessment	25 minutes
Ethical & Legal Practices	30 minutes

Strategy: Stick to a **steady pace** and use the built-in timer on the **computer-based test (CBT)** to track your progress.

3. Read Questions Carefully

- Watch for **keywords** like **"BEST," "MOST," "EXCEPT," and "NOT"**, as these can **change the meaning of the question**.

- Eliminate **obviously incorrect** answers before selecting the best one.

- If a question seems **unclear**, reread it and look for **clues in the wording**.

Example:

Which of the following **is NOT** a legally required component of an IEP?

A) Present Levels of Performance

B) Annual Goals

C) Student's Home Address

D) Special Education Services

Correct Answer: C) Student's Home Address (irrelevant to an IEP).

4. Use the Process of Elimination (POE)

- **Eliminate incorrect options** to **narrow down choices**.

- Even if you don't know the exact answer, removing wrong answers increases your **chances of selecting the correct one**.

Example:

What is the primary purpose of **a Functional Behavior Assessment (FBA)**?

A) To diagnose a student with a specific learning disability

B) To determine the function of a student's behavior and develop interventions

C) To create a lesson plan for the student

D) To evaluate a teacher's classroom management skills

Correct Answer: B) To determine the function of a student's behavior and develop interventions.

Strategy: If unsure, eliminate the least likely answers and make an educated guess—there is no penalty for guessing!

5. Recognize Common Question Types

- **Scenario-Based Questions** – These require applying **teaching strategies, laws, or classroom management techniques** to real-life situations.

- **Definition Questions** – These assess your understanding of key **terms, disabilities, or educational laws**.

- **Best-Practice Questions** – These test your knowledge of **effective teaching strategies and ethical considerations**.

Example of a Scenario Question:

A student with autism becomes overwhelmed by loud noises in the cafeteria and has frequent meltdowns. What is the best **classroom strategy** to support this student?

A) Have the student stay in the cafeteria without modifications

B) Allow the student to eat in a quieter area with noise-reducing headphones

C) Require the student to socialize with all classmates during lunch

D) Ignore the behavior and expect the student to adapt

Correct Answer: B) Allow the student to eat in a quieter area with noise-reducing headphones.

Strategy: Think about **what benefits the student most** while ensuring compliance with **best practices in special education**.

☐ 6. Double-Check Your Work

- If time allows, **review flagged questions** and ensure there are no **skipped answers**.

- **Trust your first instinct**—unless you find strong evidence to change an answer, stick with your initial response.

Strategy: Save at least **5-10 minutes at the end of the exam** for a quick review.

Overcoming Test Anxiety

Many test-takers struggle with **test anxiety**, which can negatively affect **performance and confidence**. Here's how to manage it:

1. Prepare Mentally and Physically

- **Get plenty of rest** the night before the exam.

- Eat a **healthy, protein-rich meal** before the test to maintain focus.

- Stay **hydrated** but avoid excessive caffeine to prevent jitteriness.

Strategy: Treat test day like **a normal, productive day**—don't over-stress!

2. Build Confidence Through Practice

- Take **multiple practice tests** under timed conditions to **simulate the real exam experience**.

- Review **common mistakes** and learn from them to improve.

Strategy: The more you practice, the more comfortable and confident you'll feel!

3. Use Relaxation Techniques

If you feel nervous, try:

✔ **Deep Breathing** – Inhale for 4 seconds, hold for 4 seconds, and exhale for 4 seconds.

✔ **Progressive Muscle Relaxation** – Tighten and relax each muscle group for a calming effect.

✔ **Positive Visualization** – Picture yourself **answering questions confidently and passing the exam**.

Strategy: Before starting the test, take a **moment to breathe and focus**—this can **reduce stress and improve concentration**.

4. Stay Positive and Avoid Negative Thinking

- Replace thoughts like **"I will fail"** with **"I am prepared and capable."**

- Focus on **what you know** rather than dwelling on difficult questions.

- If you don't know an answer, **stay calm, eliminate wrong choices, and make an educated guess**.

Strategy: Your mindset impacts your performance—stay confident and **trust your preparation!**

Final Tips for Exam Day Success

Before the Exam:

✔ Review key concepts and practice test-taking strategies.

✔ Check test location, rules, and ID requirements.

✔ Get a full night's sleep and eat a nutritious meal.

During the Exam:

✔ Read each question carefully and eliminate wrong answers.

✔ Manage your time—don't spend too long on difficult questions.

✔ Stay calm and focused—use deep breathing if needed.

After the Exam:

✔ Take a moment to relax and reflect on your performance.

✔ If retaking the test, review weak areas and adjust your study plan.

✔ Celebrate your hard work!

The **Praxis Special Education: Severe to Profound (5547) Exam** is an important step toward **becoming a certified special education teacher**. With **effective preparation, strong test-taking strategies, and stress-management techniques**, you can confidently **tackle the exam and achieve success.**

ADDITIONAL RESOURCES

RECOMMENDED ONLINE RESOURCES AND ACADEMIC MATERIALS

To **maximize your preparation** for the **Praxis Special Education: Severe to Profound (5547) Exam**, it is essential to supplement this study guide with **trusted online resources, academic books, and professional organizations**. Below, you'll find **hand-picked** resources that provide **valuable insights, research-based strategies, and extra practice materials**.

Recommended Online Resources

These online platforms offer **free and paid** resources, including **practice tests, study materials, legal updates, and interactive learning tools**.

1. Official ETS Praxis Website

https://www.ets.org/praxis

- The **official source** for Praxis test information, including:
    Exam structure and content outlines
    Official study companions
    Sample questions and test-taking strategies
    Registration details and test dates

- **Best For:** Understanding the exam format and accessing **authentic** Praxis 5547 materials.

2. Council for Exceptional Children (CEC)

https://www.cec.sped.org

- A professional association for special educators that provides:
  Research articles and best practices
  Special education law updates
  Webinars, online courses, and training programs

- **Best For: Staying updated** with the latest trends and policies in special education.

3. National Center for Learning Disabilities (NCLD)

https://www.ncld.org

- Offers **in-depth resources** on learning disabilities, including:
  Research-based instructional strategies
  Parent and educator toolkits
  Advocacy support and policy updates

- **Best For:** Educators working with students with **learning disabilities and processing disorders**.

4. IRIS Center – Vanderbilt University

https://iris.peabody.vanderbilt.edu

- A **U.S. Department of Education-funded center** offering:
  Free online modules on evidence-based teaching practices
  Video case studies for **real-life classroom applications**
  Special education law and ethics training

- **Best For: Interactive learning** through case studies and **evidence-based teaching strategies**.

5. Understood.org – Special Education Support

https://www.understood.org

- Provides **resources for both educators and families**, including:
  Personalized learning plans for students with disabilities
  Assistive technology recommendations
  Behavior management strategies

- **Best For:** Practical strategies for **modifying instruction and supporting students with severe disabilities**.

6. Special Education Legal Resources □

https://www.wrightslaw.com

- A **leading resource** for understanding **special education laws**, covering:

    Individuals with Disabilities Education Act (**IDEA**)

    Section 504 & Americans with Disabilities Act (**ADA**)

    IEP development and parent advocacy

- **Best For:** Ensuring **legal compliance** in special education and learning about **IEP rights and accommodations**.

7. Free Online Practice Tests & Flashcards

- **Quizlet (https://www.quizlet.com)** – Free Praxis 5547 flashcards & study sets.

- **Mometrix (https://www.mometrix.com)** – Free sample questions & study guides.

- **Teachers Test Prep (https://www.teacherstestprep.com)** – Video lessons & practice tests.

- **Study.com (https://www.study.com)** – Praxis 5547 video lessons & study guides.

- **Khan Academy (https://www.khanacademy.org)** – General education and special education concepts.

✔ **Best For:** Reviewing key concepts through **flashcards, quizzes, and video lessons**.

Recommended Academic Books and Journals

These **books and research journals** provide **in-depth coverage** of special education principles, instructional strategies, and legal frameworks.

1. Praxis Special Education (5547) Study Guides

✔ **"Praxis Special Education (5547) Study Guide 2024-2025" – By Test Treasure Publication**

- **This study guide is the most comprehensive resource** for Praxis 5547 preparation, covering:
  Exam overview, detailed content review, and practice tests
  Test-taking strategies and IEP implementation techniques

✔ **"Praxis Special Education (5547) Exam Secrets" – By Mometrix**

- Includes **practice questions and detailed answer explanations**

✔ **"Praxis II Special Education: Core Knowledge and Applications" – By ETS**

- **Official** ETS guide with **sample questions and study strategies**

Best For: Direct **test preparation** and understanding **exam format**.

2. Special Education Instructional Strategies Books

✔ **"Teaching Students with Severe Disabilities" – By David L. Westling & Lise Fox**

- Covers **curriculum design, adaptive instruction, and classroom management** for students with severe disabilities.

✔ **"Adapting Early Childhood Curricula for Children with Special Needs"** — **By Ruth E. Cook & M. Diane Klein**

- **Practical guide** on modifying lesson plans and integrating assistive technology.

✔ **"Applied Behavior Analysis for Teachers"** — **By Paul A. Alberto & Anne C. Troutman**

- Explains **behavioral intervention techniques and classroom management**.

Best For: Expanding teaching strategies for students with severe disabilities.

3. Legal & Ethical Practices in Special Education □

✔ **"Wrightslaw: Special Education Law"** — **By Peter W.D. Wright & Pamela Darr Wright**

- A **detailed reference** on IDEA, Section 504, IEPs, and legal rights.

✔ **"The Law and Special Education"** — **By Mitchell L. Yell**

- Provides a **comprehensive overview** of special education laws.

✔ **"IEPs: Writing Quality Individualized Education Programs"** — **By G. Bateman & J. Linden**

- A step-by-step **guide to writing effective IEPs**.

Best For: Understanding legal rights and compliance in special education.

4. Research Journals for Special Education

- **Journal of Special Education (JSE)** – Research on instructional strategies.

- **Exceptional Children Journal (CEC)** – Covers **disabilities, learning techniques, and policy updates**.

- **The Journal of Autism and Developmental Disorders** – Focuses on **autism interventions**.

- **Behavioral Disorders Journal** – Discusses **classroom behavior management techniques**.

Best For: Staying updated on **research-based teaching strategies and new developments in special education**.

The resources listed here **go beyond test preparation**, offering valuable insights for **becoming a successful special education teacher**. By combining **this study guide** with **trusted online tools, academic books, and professional organizations**, you will be well-equipped to:

✔ **Pass the Praxis Special Education: Severe to Profound (5547) Exam** with confidence.
✔ **Apply research-based teaching strategies** in the classroom.
✔ **Stay legally compliant** with **special education policies**.
✔ **Support students with severe and profound disabilities** effectively.

FINAL WORDS

YOUR JOURNEY TO SUCCESS

Congratulations on making it this far in your **Praxis Special Education: Severe to Profound (5547) Exam** preparation journey! Preparing for this exam is not just about **earning a certification**—it's about **becoming a stronger advocate and educator** for students with severe and profound disabilities.

The work you are preparing to do is **life-changing**. As a special education teacher, you will **shape the futures** of students who rely on your patience, creativity, and expertise to **thrive in their learning environments**. This career is more than just a job—it is **a calling, a passion, and an opportunity to make a lasting difference**.

Remember Why You Started

✔ You are here because you believe in inclusion and equal opportunities.

✔ You are preparing for this exam because you want to be the best educator possible.

✔ Your knowledge and skills will empower students who need you the most.

Every lesson you plan, every strategy you implement, and every challenge you overcome will contribute to the **growth, independence, and success** of your students.

Overcoming Challenges: You've Got This!

Let's be honest—**studying for a major exam can feel overwhelming.** But don't let self-doubt creep in. You have already taken the **first and most important step**: committing to this journey.

A Few Reminders Before Test Day:

You have prepared well—trust your knowledge and study efforts.
Take your time, read carefully, and apply test-taking strategies.
Breathe! Stay calm and focused—anxiety is normal but manageable.
Visualize your success—see yourself passing this exam with confidence!

Even if a question seems difficult, **believe in yourself**. You have **practiced, studied, and prepared**—now it's time to show what you know.

Your Impact Goes Beyond the Exam

Passing this exam **is just the beginning** of your incredible journey in special education. Beyond certification, you will have the chance to:

Empower students to reach their full potential.
Support families in advocating for their children.

Shape inclusive classrooms where every child feels valued.
Be a lifelong learner, continuously improving your skills and knowledge.

Never forget: You are not just studying for an exam—you are preparing to change lives.

Keep Pushing Forward!

This may be **one of the most challenging exams** you've taken, but remember: **every great educator started where you are now.** The best teachers are **life-long learners** who are always growing and evolving.

Keep learning.
Keep believing in your students.
Keep believing in yourself.

You are **more than capable of passing this exam and excelling in your career.** The students who will one day sit in your classroom are waiting for an educator like you—**someone who is dedicated, compassionate, and ready to make a difference.**

When you pass this exam (and **you will!**), take a moment to celebrate . But remember—your true reward is the impact you will have on the **lives of students with severe and profound disabilities.**

EXPLORE OUR RANGE OF STUDY GUIDES

At Test Treasure Publication, we understand that academic success requires more than just raw intelligence or tireless effort—it requires targeted preparation. That's why we offer an extensive range of study guides, meticulously designed to help you excel in various exams across the USA.

Our Offerings

- **Medical Exams:** Conquer the MCAT, USMLE, and more with our comprehensive study guides, complete with practice questions and diagnostic tests.

- **Law Exams:** Get a leg up on the LSAT and bar exams with our tailored resources, offering theoretical insights and practical exercises.

- **Business and Management Tests:** Ace the GMAT and other business exams with our incisive guides, equipped with real-world examples and scenarios.

- **Engineering & Technical Exams:** Prep for the FE, PE, and other technical exams with our specialized guides, which delve into both fundamentals and complexities.

- **High School Exams:** Be it the SAT, ACT, or AP tests, our high school range is designed to give you a competitive edge.

- **State-Specific Exams:** Tailored resources to help you with exams unique to specific states, whether it's teacher qualification exams or state civil service exams.

Why Choose Test Treasure Publication?

- **Comprehensive Coverage:** Each guide covers all essential topics in detail.

- **Quality Material:** Crafted by experts in each field.

- **Interactive Tools:** Flashcards, online quizzes, and downloadable resources to complement your study.

- **Customizable Learning:** Personalize your prep journey by focusing on areas where you need the most help.

- **Community Support:** Access to online forums where you can discuss concerns, seek guidance, and share success stories.

Contact Us

For inquiries about our study guides, or to provide feedback, please email us at support@testtreasure.com.

Order Now

Ready to elevate your preparation to the next level? Visit our website www.testtreasure.com to browse our complete range of study guides and make your purchase.

Made in the USA
Monee, IL
08 May 2025

17087992R00133